# Explore the Sacred

# Through Geometry

Sacred Geometry defined; why and how to create your own.

Paul Stang, M.A.

Illustration credits are noted on the pictures, throughout the book.

Printed on Createspace

Stang, Paul

Explore the Sacred through Geometry / by Paul Stang

ISBN 978-0578029092

# Foreward

What is Sacred Geometry? In the first book by this author; "We as Architects in the Wheel of Life", a great deal of space was expended in showing the mathematical concepts with which Humans measure time, distance, and volume, and how these relate to somewhat common, and often ubiquitous religious or otherwise meaningful Human – created symbols. We saw the mathemagic of Phi and other numbers like $\sqrt{2}$, $\sqrt{3}$, and $\sqrt{5}$. There were shown the relationships between trigonometry and astrology, planetary spacing and the Human body, and regular forms, which are rigidly held to the same numeric (non-random) values.

Part of the "definition" of what is Sacred Geometry is contained in no small part in these relationships, in the hard – concrete mathematics, in that which is around us, "hidden" and seen. The math, the numbers, are unfortunately exhausting for many people. Unfortunate because mathematics as it has been taught has been anything but exciting and so the people who could extract perhaps the most from it have early on been repelled by what they thought it to be.

In the classroom we have dispelled a lot of fears and allergies to math, through use of a myriad of methods. We have found wonder! Students have made discovery and become thrilled to see what mathematics has been and could truly be. The automatons who excel in the "normal" classroom are challenged to get themselves out of the box and develop – perhaps harder than enabling the rest of the class to become enthusiastic for the subject.

All of the material in We as Architects is proven. Teachers, Home-schooling parents, and Directors of alternative schools around the world are becoming aware of this new-old material and are gaining interest. People from the general public want to know: "What is Sacred Geometry and wow; I wish I'd learned mathematics like this in school".

After only one year, interest in the book and associated talks and workshops have inspired a revised copy and this totally new effort; a companion volume in which specific drawing techniques are given, so that explorers see step-by-step how to begin and are given ideas how to then proceed in creating their own Sacred Geometry; particularly through the meditational practice of drawing and coloring mandalas and then the creation of three dimensional forms.

The intention here is to discuss Sacred Geometry pictorially, as Jan Amos Commenius might have done four centuries ago. The instruction flows, from start to finish in approximately the order in which it can logically be taught and presented (as dictated by a dozen years of teaching specifically this).

In the process of writing We as Architects, there was a desire to spread the topic even further, into the realm of metaphysics. But that book is aimed at presenting creative educational techniques. Linking it also to spirituality could possibly be going too far. However, a year of presenting the book to a mixed audience has shown that many adults want to know about deeper meanings.

We are post modernists. The tallest buildings in towns and cities used to be the cathedral or mosque. Today, less attractive constructions reach much higher.

What new can come to fill an ever growing spiritual gulf that many feel today? Retrenching in the old? Experimentation with something new? Bahai? Wicca? Angels and Faeries? Perhaps the dawning of the Age of Aquarius is fertile ground, just as the time of Jesus saw Mithraism, Gnosticism, Zoroastrianism and other beliefs spawn and unite with Christianity, as it also absorbed many of its sires.

In this techno-information age invention encourages forgetfulness, even dullness. Info is not in reality wisdom. Many like to act and think that they are "knowledgeable", but might be highly ignorant, childish-boorish in thinking themselves to be wise when they are only scratching the surface. How do we use information for deepening understanding of universality? And how do we survive this explosion of techno-info?

In this time, we have unprecedented access to information and it shows that external structures to whom we've given over our power in the past are corrupted at best, and at worst leaderless. We are now called upon to find the power within ourselves. Too, we can see, touch, and experience theology from other cultures much more than any have been able to in the past. This means that the New World Order need not be secular, monetarily driven, violent, nor dictated or sold to us.

Truly, the information may be overwhelming at times; is broad, shallow, and rapid; surrounded by commercials, pop-ups, dancing advertisement windows, unexpected porn; and burdened by malfunction, interruption, and tangled cables (or the worse psychic mess of wireless). *Chaos*. The Rush of the Modern is rapid, and is rapidly accelerating. Our bodies, minds, and consciousness are tasked with surviving this largely unconscious evolution. Some may go to escapism/addiction, or find relief through activity. Or we can draw, meditate, and breathe, perhaps finding in ancient streams, and in Self, sustainability.

This book is about drawing form, understanding certain mathematical/magical precepts and finding this in our natural and Human created world, particularly in symbols. What is buried within our psyche, from which our Modern Mind is long departed? How could a sense of this bring us back to center? How do symbols, number, and mandala play a role in our past, present, and future?

As we find the time for this work, our life and our greater world changes.

It should be noted early on that the chapters in this book are uniquely numbered. The reason for this should become obvious as we progress. Going 1-2-3... is not the best sequence in seeking to create, and understand Sacred Geometry. To do so there are key number patterns, vibrations, or frequencies that we should study.

There is a spiritual essence filling all things. Omniscience is omnipresent. Within the realm of the immortals, the 12 (or 8) archetypes, and among the angelic, spiritual, and physical planes there is Mind.

Let's proceed slowly to learn further. Hopefully it can be excused if the wording at times seems too leading. It is after all written by a school teacher.

I saw you when you wandered but, my dear son, I wanted no longer to wait for you; so I brought you to yourself and into your own heart – Comenius, Labyrinth of the World
1631

We exist in a multi-dimensional reality and we can access other dimensions in various ways – Francene Hart

# Table of Contents

sm

Dances of Universal Peace

This book is dedicated to those who have asked for its creation, to those who are dedicating themselves to bringing the Light into our World, and of course for Anna Marie who I cherish and for whom I hope to do my part in building a more positive future.

> When I see the sun
>  I think God's spirit
> When I use my hand
>  God's soul lives in me
> When I take a step
>  God's will walks in me
> And when I see other people
>  God's soul lives in them
>              Rudolf Steiner –
>                  Prayers for Mothers and Children

# First Chapter – 6

What is Sacred Geometry?  What can be Sacred about Geometry?  Is the Sacred not the realm of religions?  Certainly religious buildings, of merit, are often geometric wonders.  Their authors incorporated proportion such that sound resonates within, and brought in colored glass in geometrically shaped windows to draw in and diffuse the light of the sun for the worshippers.  In the East, those temples of the Diety are particularly alive with colorful geometric design, often without iconography.

But the secular world also contains numerous examples of very similar construction, like the capitol buildings within each of the United States, the Taj Mahal, the Forbidden City, and various world parliaments.

The skyscrapers of the early 20th century, rather unexciting boxes, have evolved to crystalline constructions of glass and steel, in a never-ending procession of building.  Yet, more attractive geometric construction endures, not to be torn down, as witnessed by the pyramids around the world, stone circles, and other ancient constructions still with us after millennia.

In these 60 or so centuries of classical geometric construction certainly the study of natural laws was much different than our industrialized world of the last 2 centuries can comprehend.  If we could somehow shed the veil that industry and technology have enshrouded us with we might be able to appreciate more what Pythagoras, Kepler, and many others have attempted to explore.

The Sacred is all around us.  It can be geometrical... mathematical.  It is contained in the Human, in Number, in Tone and in Color.  We will begin to make it, think about what we are creating, and how it relates to us.

Figure 1, Mystical geometric diagram.  A. Kircher  ars magna sciendi 17th century.

Our journey of discovery begins best in the same place, be it individually or at university, adult workshop, high-school, grade-school, and even kindergarten:  the Circle.

With the youngest child we find they are happy to make contact, to hold hands and to make a circle. Even a group of adults, complete strangers can accept this as an introduction (with or without the handholding); as a way to "break the ice". Why are we so comfortable with joining as a circle?

Let's form one with our selves, and others. What do we notice? We see everybody. Someone stands directly opposite us. It's fun! What happens if we stretch our arms as far as they can go? The circle gets larger. How do we make it the smallest possible circle? We bring our arms in until our shoulders touch.

Let's draw a circle. First, tie a piece of chalk on a string, have someone hold the rope on one place, and a second stretch the rope and draw on the floor as they walk around the first. It will make the same type of shape as perhaps the earliest circle makers inscribed thousands of years ago.

What is unique about a circle? No beginning or end. Only continuity. All points are an equal distance from the center. Imagine all of us as a part of that circle. Look to the nighttime sky. What does the full moon look like? A circle. What is it in reality? A sphere. Ah....

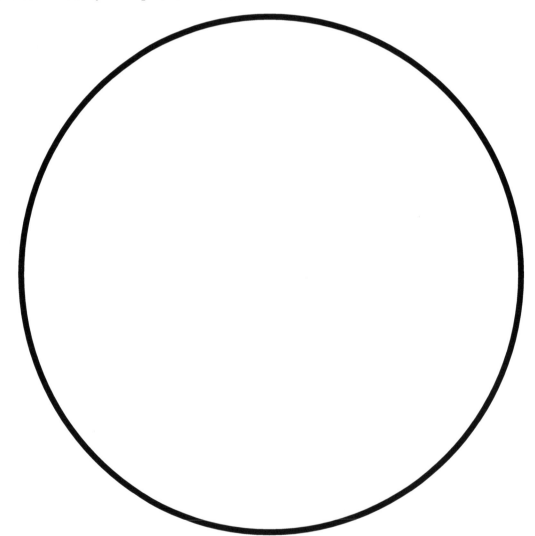

Figure 2, The perfection of the circle.

Use the circle drawn on the floor. Stand and walk along it, as though it is a tight rope. Remain quiet and walk heal-to-toe. This is a good practice in balance and more is a most relaxing meditation.

Now, how could we make a smaller circle? The rope has to be shorter. Ok, how do they get it to fit exactly in the original (concentric)?

The next thing to do is to create a rudimentary compass. For this we need two pieces of string and two sticks. Let's tie the sticks together at one end so they cross and are somewhat free to pivot. Or break a fresh stick, retaining outward tension. Take the other string and tie it to each stick, all as shown in Figure 3a.

Try using this to draw circles in the dirt. How could we make a different sized circle? By varying the second string length. Play with this.

This rudimentary compass can be refined to include a dull point on one stick and a pencil attached to the other so that we can expand the "technology" and the technique in order to draw a circle on paper.

We move then to a real compass. It's understood that some people need more time in becoming familiar with the device (particularly pre-teens), seeing the need for precision and how to develop it, and wanting to obtain that precision.

## Introduction

Throughout this book, many pages will show in miniature key steps needed to create an image; a completed form of which will be given immediately beneath, usually an enlarged version.

The key is to do these mostly in the order presented from beginning to end of this book, as this is the sequence which has been shown to work best in developing understanding. Don't simply copy the images and color them. Don't opt for doing them on the computer. Sure, once a person has done hundreds or more, they can use technology to try ideas, to see what might or might not look good or to practice color usage. But each beginner, those intentionally or accidentally finding the process meditational, and the most advanced student wishing to create true art, needs to draw; finding out how to pirouette the compass in just two fingers so it dances like a ballerina. They need to get graphite on their fingers, learn precision, erase mistakes, or erase to enhance certain features. They should color with pencils, markers, and paints, and use different kinds, sizes, and colors of paper. They need to enjoy the process of creation, the frustration of dissatisfaction, the boredom that breaks down walls to new realms. This effort encompasses part of what is sacred in Sacred Geometry.

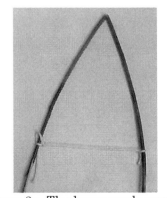
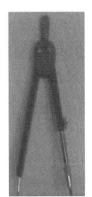

Figure 3a, The home-made compass.          Figure 3b, Good beginner and advanced compasses.

The compass we obtain should be a little costly depending upon interest and maturity. A simpler (less sharp!) version should be given juniors but absolutely not one of the cheap ones, which generally don't hold the pencil well or retain their radial size. These supposed "safe" compasses result in a frustrating process for the novice as their "circle" opens with rotation, creating a sort of spiral, the pencil slips or another problem occurs. A suitable compass can be had for less than $5. Just have a small screw-driver handy to tighten up the device so it holds well as circles are made.

**The Daisy**

Our first "scientific" step in developing an understanding of Sacred Geometry is to draw a circle; here of radius 2-4 inches (2-4"). The standard system is used throughout this book because of its tremendous relationship to Sacred Geometry. Metric? Should the reader prefer the metric system then using an appropriate adjustment is in order. It cannot be underestimated however the need to think hexa – decimally. For that the English system is key, as will be seen.

Make a top mark on this circle and then draw from there a second ring of equal size (Figures 4).

Turn the paper sidewise, and we see two circles joined as partners. This image is called the Vesica Piscis. Very similar in name to Pisces, we are reminded of duality, partnership. In mathematics this image can be used to explain many concepts. It has been identified as a simple layout tool possibly used by the master craftsmen when they constructed the great gothic cathedrals.

Rotate the paper back to the original configuration. Where this second circle crosses the first (on each side of it) place the compass point and draw an additional circle, maintaining the same compass size (radius). Use the places where these two new circles intersect as centers of another pair. Draw a final (6th) circle at the bottom.

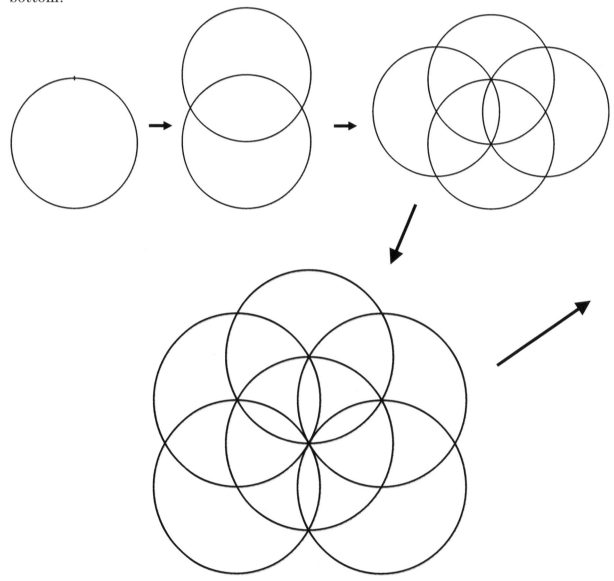

Figure 4a, Beginning steps, of a long journey of understanding.

Figure 4b, the "daisy".

Our daisy is called by some the "flower of life". This phraseology tells us that we are not merely drawing random forms without higher meaning.

Now, check for precision, as shown in Figure 5. Then do a further ring of circles to practice precision, and develop some ideas.

Figure 5, Check precision: Crisp intersections at six places around the initial circle. At its center see that all curves come together tangentially (meeting at only one place).

To begin building the second set of circles, use the six outer intersections found on our initial drawing. The meeting of each pair of new circles, at a daisy tip, indicate an additional six points from which to generate the last circles (Figure 6).

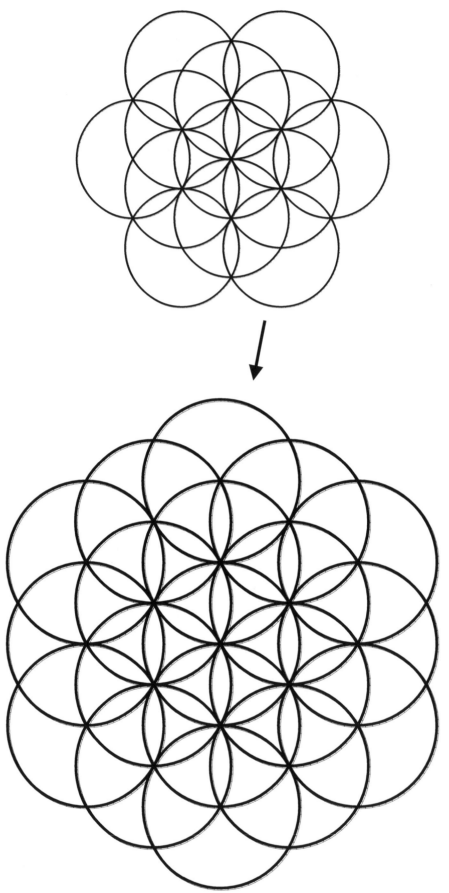

Figure 6, Complete the outer set of circles.

Thus we have created now the "tree of life". Count the number of circles in the first "circuit" (6) and then in the second (12). See if precision has been maintained. Notice the overall shape (hexagonal).

## Mandala

To learn about sacred geometry, we should try to draw some! What makes our own drawing sacred? The fact that we ourselves, our unique consciousness, made it. This is the creating of mandalas.

The process of geometric drawing is one of experimentation, thought, and ultimately meditation. This is what could be described as *being* Mandala. The term itself is said to mean "having essence", or perhaps "circle" or "wheel". The most important thing to keep in mind is that this "wheel" is a form of geometric art found not just in India but ubiquitously in East – West cultures; be it the medicine wheel of the indigenous Americans, cathedral roses of Europe, pagoda roofs in China, or other such examples.

Drawing and coloring a mandala is meditative; relaxing. So is looking upon the finished product.

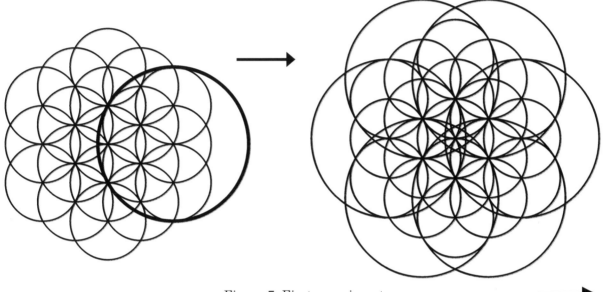

Figure 7, First experiment.

The left image in Figure 7 is generated by doubling the original compass size and placing six enlarged circles around the first. This is only one experimental route which can be taken...

This new set of larger circles, by intersecting the initial effort, creates secondary images contained within the whole. We can think immediately of how to uniquely color, or shade, these. Too, perhaps we could start to think of erasing certain lines in order to "clean up" the image. The following figures present a few possible solutions.

The key thing in drawing mandala is that lines do not come from random points in space but that they are generated from points defined within the form itself.

Figure 8a, Filling in a few of the images found on our Mandala

Figure 8b, Other options, other shades or colors to be used.

We see in Figure 8d how erasure lends us the central "folded" petal effect. This is a brilliant item to play with. The steps in doing so require a lot of circles, using two sizes; one exactly double the other. It is best to do these lightly for a great deal of erasure will occur. Conversely, these can be darkly drawn (in ink) as a permanent model for work to be done later, should the artist then wish to overlay a finer (semi-transparent) paper on top, which they will be using for their finished work (not so practical with water colors).

8

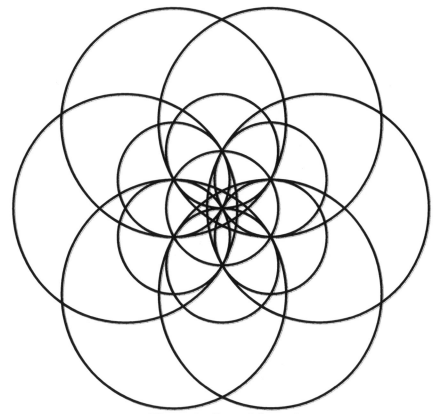

Figure 8c, Less "clutter"

Figure 8d, Some unique erasure.

When we erase, we want to use an eraser that won't mar the paper, leave smudges, or some type of residue, which may affect the quality and evenness of the colors to then be used. Particularly for water colors, eraser "technology" can be a real issue!

Figure 9a, Erasure gives possible images.

Figure 9b, Further possibility, nice in green and red at the season

Let's let the compass dance once again.  Erasure provides for creation of the "Sun". (Draw lightly)

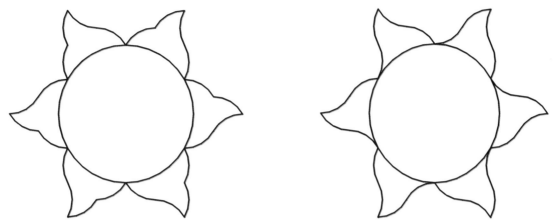

Figure 9c, Two possible sun motifs.

Sentient Life on Earth may believe in God, may worship this God under a variety of names, and use a variety of symbols to do so.  All life depends on the Sun and for this it is perhaps understandable that the Sun should symbolize God to so many throughout the march of history.  We may include the Sun in a geometric drawing; directly as is shown in Figures 9c and d, or we may use a stellar shape, a ringed cross as did the Irish, or merely by use of colors (yellow and orange).

Figure 9d, The Sun, or a brilliant flower form to include in a mandalic drawing.

There are countless options as we draw.  The key is to try some.  See what the compass will do at double or treble the original size.  What crossings and arcs create for special features?  What could be erased to enhance the drawing?  And then, what to do about color?  That information is coming...

We have increased the size of our compass incrementally.  What if we change its size only minutely?  In Figure 10 we see an example of our daisy with a second, smaller, daisy superimposed.  All radii are a hair smaller but centered upon the same place as the original seven circles.  Creative erasure provides the impression of rings overlapping upon each other.

If we change the size *and* shift the center, we have the possibilities in Figure 11 to consider.  In the construction diagram the original circles are slightly thinner.

Figure 10, Interweaving rings generated by concentric circles.

Figure 11, Interweaving rings with shifted centers on the circles.

## Masculine

In creating mandala, and Sacred Geometry, there is much to be considered. So far the reader should see that the pictures are symmetrical, and hence balanced. They have appeared delicate, "flowery". Their curvatiousness could be and is considered feminine. The balance that we need to embrace, in our lives and in our artwork, should include also masculine energy, considered in geometric art to consist of straight lines, and sharp points.

We will see too that color will provide further things to consider. Our next step is to revisit the basic circle, now done on a larger scale with a radius of say 4".

Draw the circle centered on the page. Make again a top mark. With the compass perform a similar set of steps as before but now only obtain tick marks on the circle. Work from both sides, checking that two arcs meet precisely at the bottom. Connect these evenly around the circle, creating the hexagon. Conversely, draw lines across the image. Check precision at the center to see that all lines cross perfectly there.

Does the reader/artist notice anything in the final product? Using the compass as a measuring tool, it can be seen that all radial lines are equal to all of the sides of the hexagon. The hexagon, dividing the circle by six, is the only figure containing this special relationship.

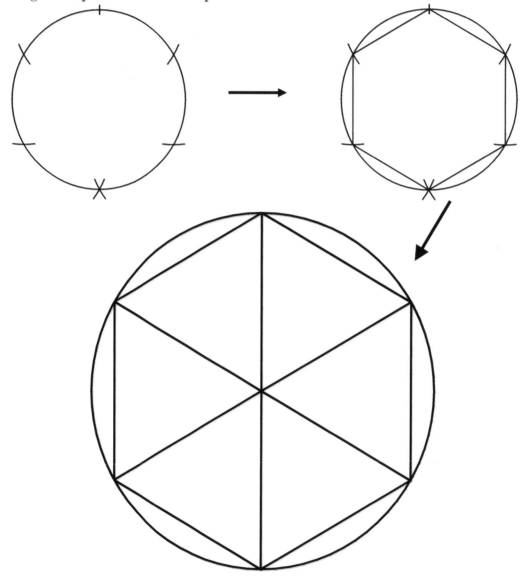

Figure 12, Hexagon with radial lines of length equaling the edges.

14

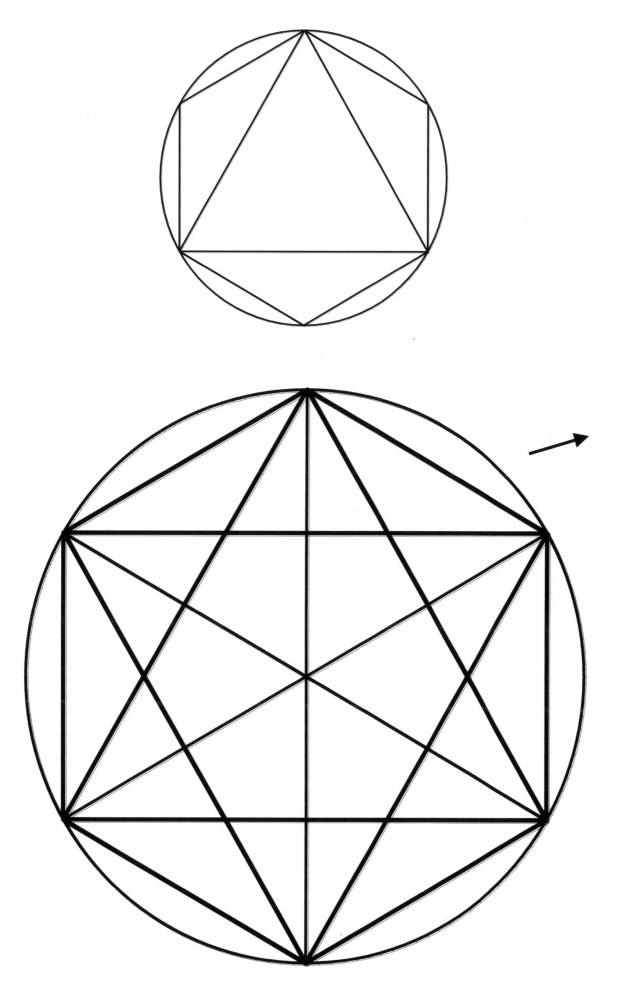

Figure 13, Optional methods of working with the Hexagon, one of them a classical symbolic figure

Figure 14a, Radial lines help see the ease of fractalization of the 6 – pointed star.

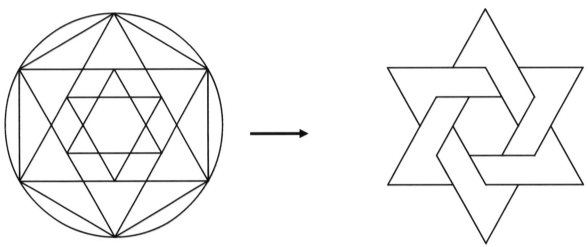

Figure 14b, Using a specific size to make a weave.

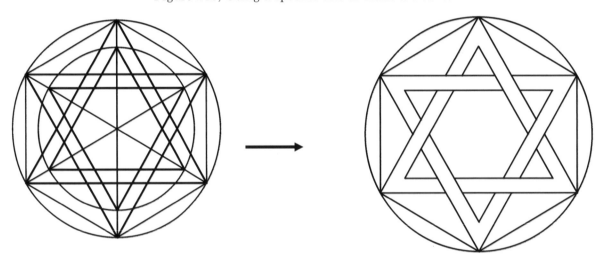

Figure 14c, Using a second, concentric circle of varied radius to make the weave.

The fractal nature of the hexagon allows for interesting drawing (and construction). Here, notice that the interweave gives the impression of motion. It seems that the stars wish to turn. Imagine the placement of such symbols within a larger drawing...

16

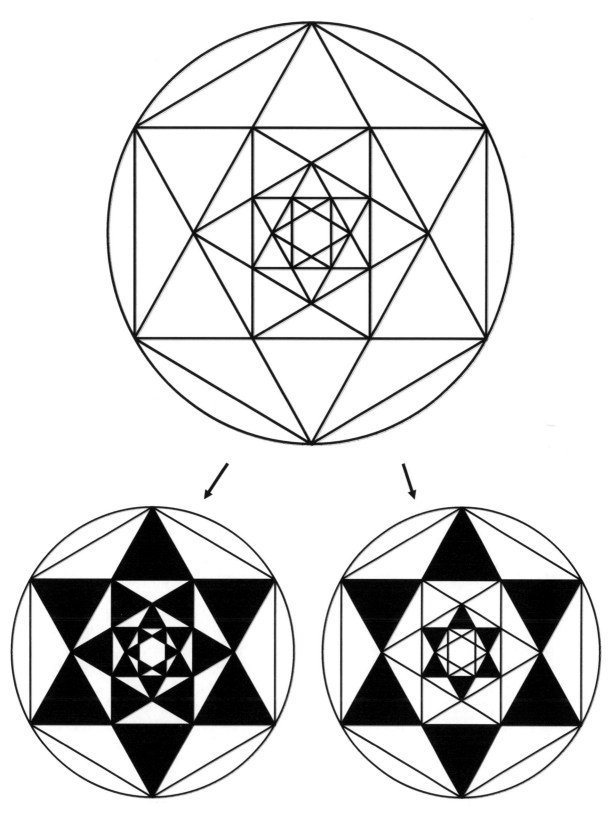

Figure 15, A different approach to the fractal (above), and various ways to color it. In the second picture, the inner white star and the outermost black star correspond quite well with the relative spacing of Earth and Jupiter around the Sun. Interesting that Jupiter's orbit is twelve years.

There is further work we can do with this star. This is a symbol held holy to one particular religion and culture on our world. And yet it can be found in art (even that which is religious in nature) across many cultures. As we study the Geometry that is Sacred, we find it repeating through time and space.

Interestingly, six – fold is readily found in nature (3 and 6 petals in flowers and leaves). Six also seems archetypal, along with five (soon to be explored!)

**The Color Wheel**

We will interrupt our work with male and female images now for it is indeed time to begin thinking of color. This was not mentioned before as the reader should have been free to experiment a little and to have been introduced to the concept of masculine/feminine balance. Before we dive into even further complexity, we will now consider color usage.

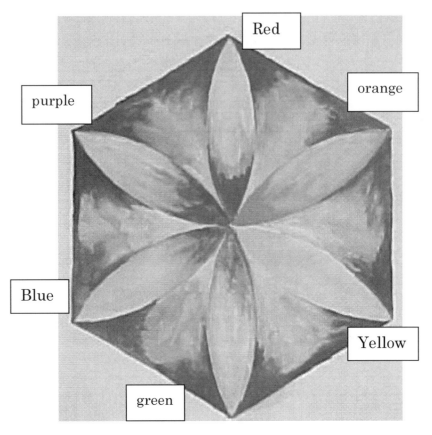

Figure 16, The color wheel (please see back cover)

Our use of color in a drawing can say a lot about us, according to color therapists. What we need to understand is that the colors we choose can enrich our creation, deplete it, or make it look like a pizza with too many toppings!

Let us first gain an understanding of colors. To begin, let's draw a daisy within a hexagon, hopefully a very doable task for the reader by now.

There are three colors considered by artists to be the primary colors: red, blue and yellow. We will place these inside three of the petals, each rotated by 120° from the other; spaced by a third of the circle. Note in Figure 16, and particularly on the back cover of this book that the petals are colored darkly at the center but ever more faintly as we proceed to the tips.

By mixing two "adjacent" primary colors, we can obtain the secondary colors. This can easily be replicated using water colors. Or, we simply place orange between red and yellow, purple between red and blue, and green between blue and yellow, again darker toward the center. The reason why the hexagon is then filled in more darkly at the extremity of the daisy is to show how to use contrasting light and dark areas next to each other to embolden the design. This also has the effect of making the image appear differently when held up close or when viewed from afar.

Shading cannot be underestimated. The tendency for the beginner is to try and use a different color for every item in the drawing. This is the overtopped pizza

18

effect that is generally not very attractive. Conversely, one could try to do their drawing with only one color! Or maybe two. Some examples are provided in miniature on the back cover. Each color can be placed onto the paper in gradations by applying firmer pressure on the pencil, or using more or less water.

Next let's consider how to use colors together. Note that either the primary or secondary colors make basically a triangle in relation to each other. This triangulation can be used to consider that such colors are thought to be complementary. It's no accident that red, white, and blue are used on many flags together.

Conversely, opposite colors on the wheel, like purple and yellow are thought to contrast, also making together an attractive image. This is why red and green at Christmas are so favorable together. Note however that in the former, we have a light color next to a darker. But, red and green are equal in weight. Watch what happens when drawing them side–by–side and then looking at them from across the room. It is hard to say where one color ends and the other begins.

Note, approximately the same means of observation can be achieved but with less walking. Squint! Look the diagram over with almost closed eyes to see how the colors go with each other. This will show if one should be darkened up and the other lightened. Sometimes a black border between the two will serve the purpose.

Finally, adjacent colors also complement, like orange with yellow and/or red. Again, try a drawing with gradations of one color, or try two or three together. Just don't try them all!

Triangular? Opposite and adjacent? Why, it sounds like one could use any color with any other. This is in fact the case. So, now we may consider the possible effect which we seek with our drawing.

Color usage is an art form in itself. Darker images in a drawing tend to stand out more, giving the figure almost a three–dimensional effect at times. Color selection can convey warmth (orange and/or red), aggression and anger (red and black), love and tranquility (green), coolness or emotion (blue), or higher thought (purple – a cross between the coolness of blue and the warmth of red).

What do the colors in our drawing wish to convey and do they achieve this? Do they show joy when we want joy? We can also think in terms of the six colors representing the first six chakras. Red is for our root. Grounding, yet also fiery and warm. Orange can be thought to represent passion, as it is associated with our sex chakra. Yellow indicates the sun; the will at our solar plexus. Green connects with the heart, blue the throat, which we open as we look up to the blue sky. Conversely, blue is thought of as cooling and is also linked with water, emotion, and depression. Finally, purple or an indigo blue can be associated with the third eye, with higher thinking. At the top of our heads, at the crown chakra could be violet, if not already used, or clear white, like a diamond or crystal.

If we, or someone with whom we are working, gravitate toward one or a few colors, this might say something about the individual. Perhaps by simply introducing other colors into the artwork that gets generated, with time the person's consciousness and life may change.

As we grow in our use and experimentation with colors, notice the clothes that people wear, or perhaps lack of colors with which they may adorn themselves. Are there any that one notices by their absence, or over use?

We need to seek balance....

As we slowly conclude this chapter, let's use the feminine to help create a masculine image. Nesting circles enables us to use points of intersection to nest hexagons (Figure 17a). Thence, a little erasure here or there provides a somewhat unique shape, as shown in Figure 17b (rotated). Looking to Figure 17c we see a different effort, where some of the lines are lightened to show their supporting role.

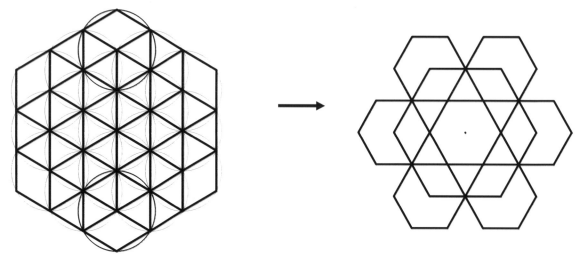

Figure 17a, Equilateral triangles and hexagons          Figure 17b,  Star of David pattern

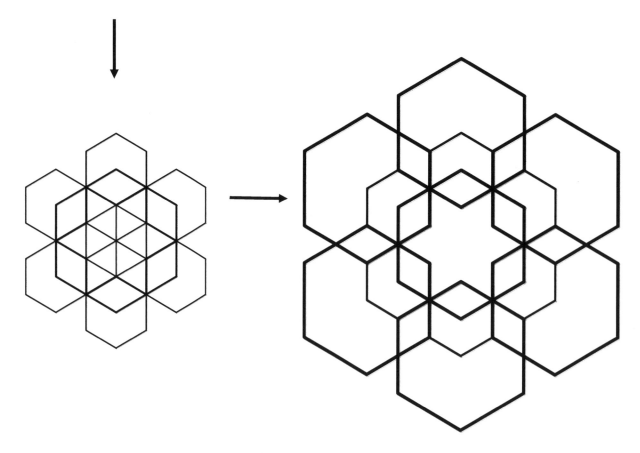

Figure 17c, Nested hexagons as a guide to larger hexagons.

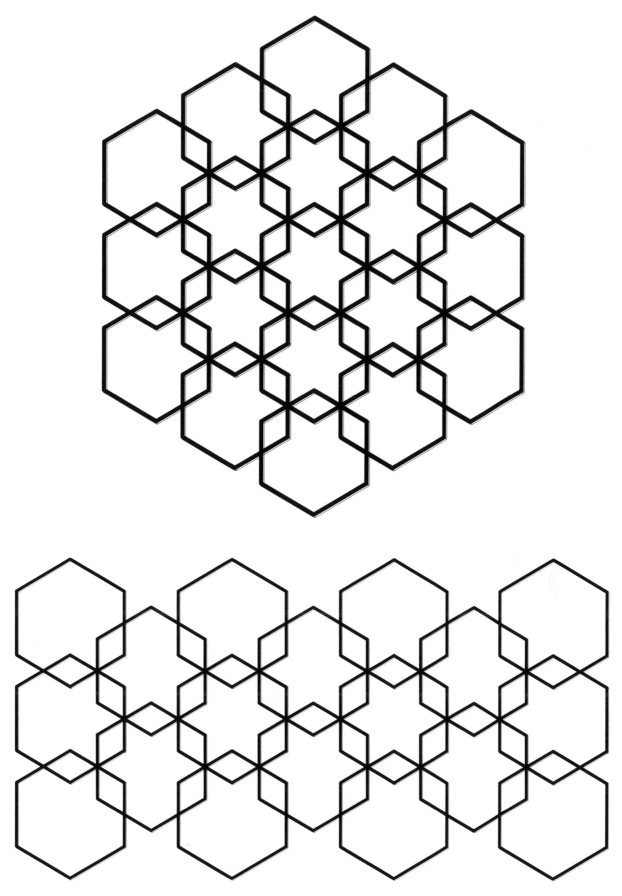

Figure 17d, Islamic tile pattern: Two views.

When we look to the symbolism of other cultures (Figure 17d), we see that though media, and others (throughout history) might try to focus on our differences, in our consciousnesses perhaps we are not so far apart.

Figure 18, Cross-cultural mystical symbolism. Secrets of Rosicrucian figures (Altona 1785-88).

Our Modern world seeks easy, quick solutions. We are so fast paced that we do not pause, give value to symbol, meditate upon it, create it; as our predecessors could afford to do. The Information of this Age does not equate to Wisdom. Facts displace. Technology enshrouds and blinds. Materialism hides us from seeking.

Let us gain insight into the Humanity of *those* Others, and find ways to resolve without destroying. Perhaps that is what the Age of Aquarius may represent.

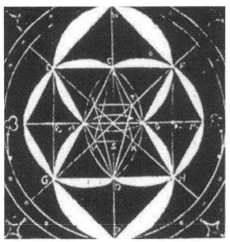

Figure 19, Articuli centrum Giordano Bruno, 1588

Bruno was a Renaissance man, born to a time when discovery and Science tried to extend the borders of understanding. Caught up in Kopernicanism, he was killed by a Church, and a world that was unwilling to accept new ideas and change, which the hierarchy could not control. We see in the piece which he created the germ of our early work here.

22

Figure 20, Typical snowflakes, all based upon six (wiki).

The crystallization of water is six – fold, just as our first stars have been. Water is the Life Bringer. No biological system can survive without it. It is also the conveyor of nutrients, the transmitter of energy, and the symbolic vessel of Spirituality.

Figure 21, Theosophical Emblem (Theosophical Glossary, 1892).

We began this chapter and will end it with the circle. This has been captured by many artists throughout history, with one example given in Figure 21, where the circle is represented by the snake eating its own tail. The Serpent, the Dragon, symbolize in many cultures death and rebirth. Shedding its skin to begin anew. The circle of life.

Figure 22, The Moon as circle and sphere (Angels guarding paradise by night. John Martin 1824).

Figure 23, Brass bowl.

## Circle meditation

Start by obtaining a good hemispherical bowl of cast iron, brass or ceramic. Hold it in your cupped hands. Notice the circular top, and the sphericity. Feel it. Earthiness.

Place inside it the purest water you can find; better one that has not touched plastic.

Call in the cosmic Essence (your God) to bless the water. Welcome not only each other but also higher consciousness and entities (Angels). Thus prepared, wash your hands and face lightly. Have those of your community, which you have been able to gather, do likewise.

It may be that you will do this work alone; All One. Revel then in your time and Self. Remember that you are however never alone.

Light candles. Imagine the fire without mirrored by that which is within. Think of the Sun, too brilliant to gaze upon.

Place symbols that you feel to be Holy around the circle which you create before you. Accept those which Others hold dear. If a group, gather round the circle. If All One, place yourself inside it. Stand beneath the celestial orbs.

Begin to chant, or sing:

> You are here, I see you
> I hear you, I feel your presence
> Come and Be with me
> Come unto this Ring,
> Bring your light, bring your Being.

> I am here, you see me
> you hear me, you feel me here with you
> Come and Be with me
> Come into the circle,
> Bring your light, come inside.

Imagine bringing cosmic light into your space, into yourself. Breathe. Bring in the Light. Be in the light. The circle is one of Gold, a ring. Enrich yourself in your own goldenness. Heal through your Auric fields.

We all know about the darkness; anger and depression. Let images of all you have seen and felt come and then let them go, particularly the ones which cause a state of unwellness within. Imagine a land upon which the sun is shining, birds are singing, and children are laughing and playing.

Go into your body and ask it, "What do I need to release? What can I heal within myself today?

Form a circle with your lips. Say, chant, sing, from deep within your belly. Ohhhhh.... Ohmmmmm....

> The Temple is before us.
> The Temple is Within.
> The Kingdom of God is around us.
> The Kingdom of God is within.

> Angels watch over us.

24

# Second Chapter – 12

Our work continues... We have begun a process in the first chapter; to solve a riddle. A complete answer to the question of what is Sacred Geometry cannot be found on the internet, nor in books (even such as this one), in travel to sacred places around the globe, or in attendance at lectures. Bits are what we find. With time, meditation, drawing, and creating (and doing some math☺), this process will awaken the individual until they simply know that they know what the answer is.

The book; "We as Architects", was part of the author's own individual process of awakening. It documents much of the science that has been re-discovered upon one person's path; from books, internet searches, a myriad of sacred places, and time in the classroom. This science has enabled said author to grasp just what is Sacred about Geometry, about Mathematics, and about Real Education.

Perhaps in lieu of all of this (years!), there are teachers who can adequately convey an understanding. Maybe there are those who are just more perceptive and can realize early on, intuitively or otherwise, what is Sacred about Geometry and why. For the author it took a transformation from a limiting educational and cultural background, which most of us experience, to open up, to begin drawing; mandala after mandala, sitting beside a peaceful river on summer journeys. It meant slowing down. It required teaching the same processes through mathematics, year after year, weaning away from the technology (the calculator) and working with just number.

There are many great books on Sacred Geometry. That now in the reader's hands is meant as a singular approach to this topic, from among the excellent material available, because here one may see fascinating images which can ultimately be created (many of which have varying degrees of difficulty), a logical sequence of steps to follow in this process, and concepts to consider.

These are steps which are proven to flow quite well. Let's revisit Figure 4 in the First Chapter. We will draw again the daisy, and this time look critically at how we can overlay 6 axial lines.

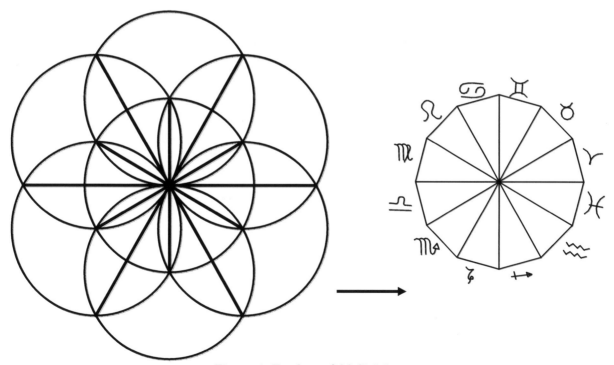

Figure 1, Twelve – fold division.

Division of the circle by twelve opens a much wider range of possibilities and is subliminally very familiar. Our minds are geared toward twelve. We count hours in two sets of twelve. Nearly all of us know which of twelve astrological signs we were born under (a common thread between East – West and over thousands of years of history). We count twelve months. We count seconds and minutes in 5 x 12. We measure our circles, and thus latitude and longitude, in 5 x 6 x 12 degrees. We measure our square and rectangular homes with the same summary angle, and halve it in our triangles. If one wonders why we measure a circle by 360 instead of 100 then see how many numbers multiply to make each. In the former there are 2 x 12 and in the latter just 10. In the west we count in do–zen (two–ten = twelve). Human psyche has long been tuned to twelve: 12 apostles, 12 Olympian Gods. In the East; 5 x 12 years in a Chinese great cycle, 12 meridians in the body. Further, 2 x 12 letters, runes, or hieroglyphs in various alphabets, 12 inches in a foot, and 440 x 12 feet in a mile. Finally, some researches believe that everything of a physical nature emits a spectrum of energy which is twelve-fold.

Let's work with 12. Figure 1 readily opens itself to the following. See in Figure 2 how to use the twelve radial lines, with alternating hexagons centered at the midpoint of each prior hex. This exercise is the next progression from our very good beginning in the previous chapter. Here, we go inward. The time taken, the concentration given will definitely slow the practitioner down, and provide focus.

Figure 2, The spider web. Only a beginning!

How next to proceed? Imagine coloring this image with one of the various options shown under Figure 3. Use of only one or two colors, with a variety of depth in those colors is usually best.

26

Figure 3a, The more common approaches to filling in Figure 2.

The dodecagon, easily divisible by a variety of numbers, is a great source for mandala work. Twelve is a harmonic with which we are very familiar. The form itself can be readily intersected by hexagons, squares, and equilateral triangles.

27

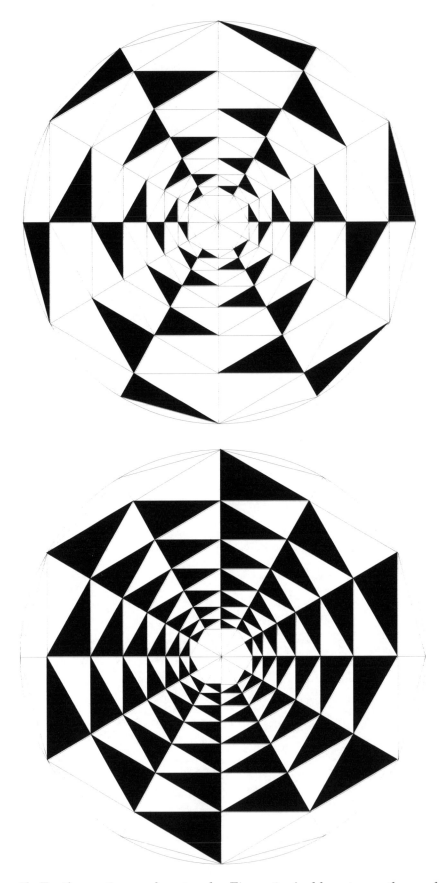

Figure 3b, Further options on how to color Figure 2. And how to use those colors?

The process of drawing and then coloring these forms is meticulous and very meditational. Note the "movement" that each contains.

The dodecagon can be seen to relate with ("birth" almost) the hex, square, and triangle. See in the images how each of the shapes are complementary.

28

With the dodecagon, we may produce a set of squares, rotated around its center. This interesting pattern, aligned with radiating axial lines provides for another "web" design, as shown in the diagrams on this page.

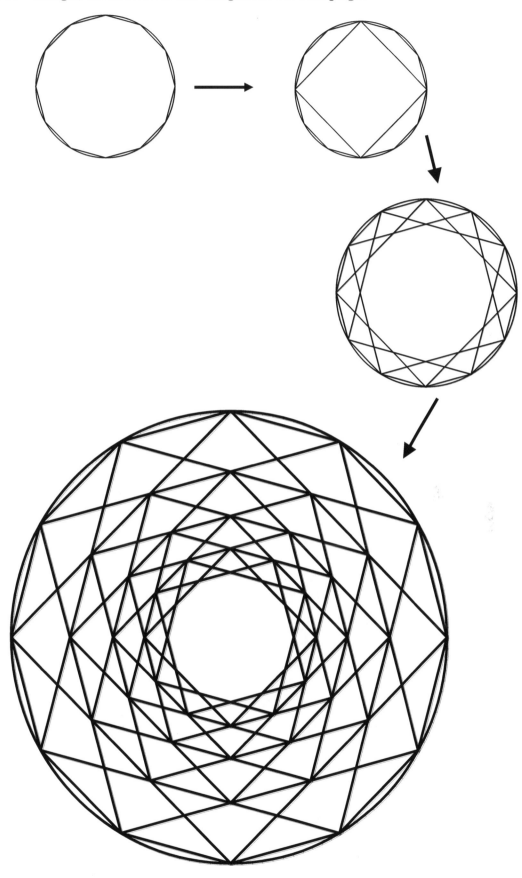

Figure 4, Web pattern based on squares and the dodecagon.

Figure 5, Possible patterns and schemes from Figure 4.

We can also work with equilateral triangles, as the next diagrams demonstrate.

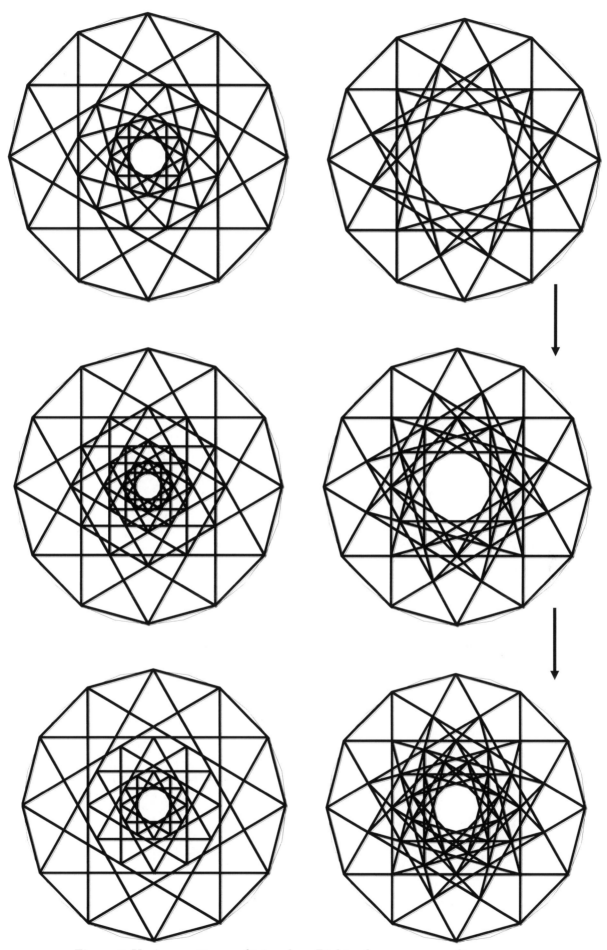

Figure 6, Various patterns of triangles. Right-column an expanding sequence.

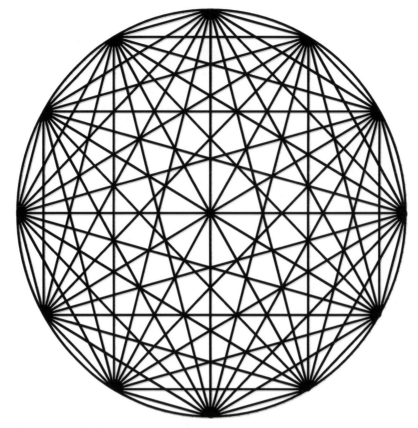

Figure 7a, Spokes radiating out from every point of the dodecagon.

At some point, many of us seem tempted to create the image in Figure 7a. Drawing radiant lines from each of the twelve vertices attracts many an artist. The form itself is indeed attractive (and also quite "busy"). We may look at it to try and find any shapes that call to us. Thus begins the task of erasing.

There is also the option of doing the lines in different colors, and not just in pen or pencil. Waldorf students have been observed to do an interesting process where they used a board into which were driven twelve equally spaced nails. For the longest "paths", they strung a red thread, looping this around the twelve points as shown in Figure 7b. The next diagram shows lines of a slightly lesser length. For this, the color orange is used. This is appropriate as the star shape created can indeed be thought to symbolize the Sun. Note here that counting clockwise or counter clockwise results in a count of 5 or 7. If we count every four points around our dodecagon, we create equilateral triangles, as shown in Figure 7d. These are done in yellow and though all are black and white here, their true beauty may be seen on the back cover. There are four triangles.

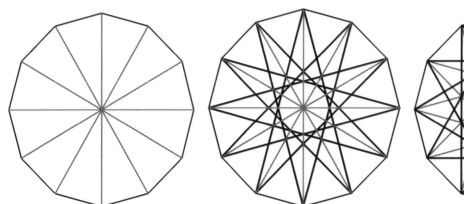

Figure 7b, Red lines across.     7c, The orange star – the Sun.     7d, Three triangles, in yellow.

Counting between each three points on the dodecagon provides a square form. There are three of these. If we link each second point we create a hexagon (two of them). The forms, shown in Figures 7e and f are done in green and blue respectively. Ultimately, the outer dodecagon is purple. We use the color wheel thusly, with a fire shown in the center, and coolness to the extremities. If we observe the Mucha stain glass in the cathedral in Prague (shown in We as Architects), we see a similar effect having been generated by the artist.

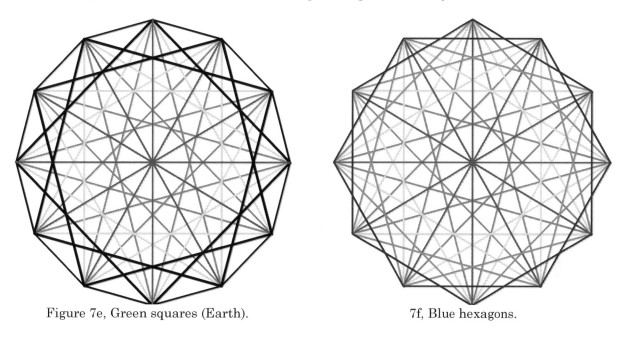

Figure 7e, Green squares (Earth).                    7f, Blue hexagons.

(see back cover)

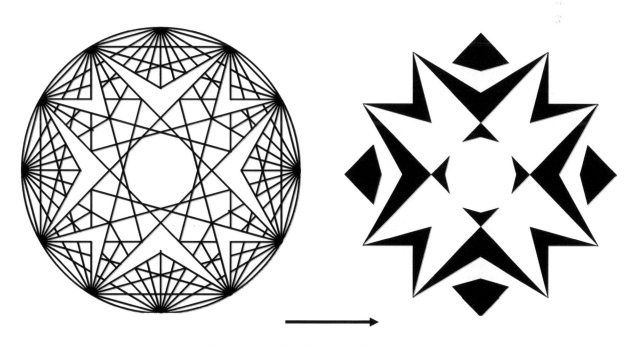

Figure 7g, Further use of Figure 7a.

We conclude this current series of work by demonstrating possible erasure and fill of our "explosion" of lines.

Figure 7h, Stars.

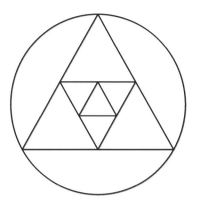

Figure 8a, Triangle Fractal.

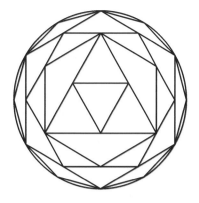

Figure 8b, Harmonics of 3–, 6–, and 12– fold forms.

Figure 8a shows further fractal possibilities, easy to make now with greater understanding. Figure 8b provides a combination of twelve– , six– , and three– fold geometries combined. It should be seen that these are all harmonious in how they fit together. Harmony, visual and musical, is a key component of Sacred Geometry.

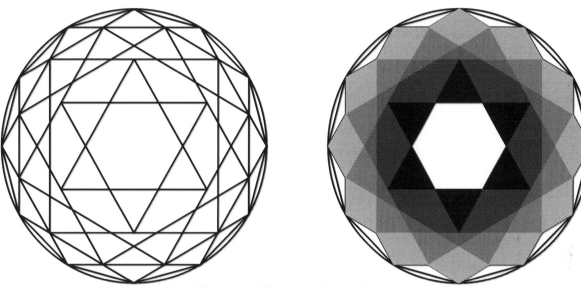

Figures 9, The many faceted gem.

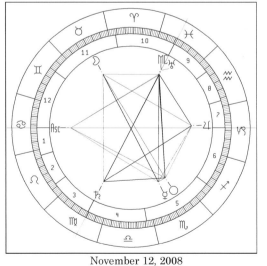

November 12, 2008                    August 11, 1999

Figure 10, Astrological charts showing interesting geometries.

Twelve – fold geometry has long guided the inexorable development of Astrology. Figure 10 demonstrates a few charts, with unique geometries of study.

### Rounding out

We now transition from the linear, back to the circular, breathing in and breathing out, letting the waves roll in, seeing the tide carry outward. Image as metaphor.

How would our life and perspective be different when in a geodesic dome, yurt, or other round dwelling?

Figure 11, Not everyone lives in a rectangular world. Tipi, Yurt, and Rondavel
(George Catlin 1846, Adagio – wiki, J. Mcdonald)

As was mentioned earlier, straight lines are generally thought to relate to masculine energy, though historic study of number might indicate that even and odd might also tend toward one gender or the other. So many nuances to consider in our art. But, on the path of the Sacred, should there not be?

Figure 12, Further ideas with curves and twelve.

Figure 12 is an example of what we can accomplish with a bit more effort. Our art is beautiful. Its creation, perfection, and display gives us pleasure and something more. It requires Mindfulness, as we make a regular pattern, seeking precision and symmetry. How we fill, erase, and color the forms can give them a completely different meaning, and can leave them stationary or provide a sense of rotary motion. With color we can emote eros, calm, or aggression. The next time one looks at a cathedral rose's beautiful stain–glass, or gazes upon a mandala, perhaps the artist's deeper intentions can be guessed at.

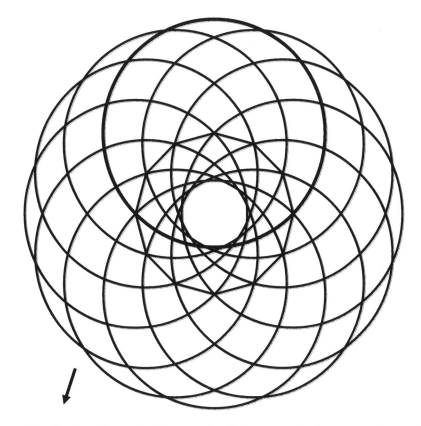

Figure 13a, Twelve circles built around a dodecagon; their centers the vertices.

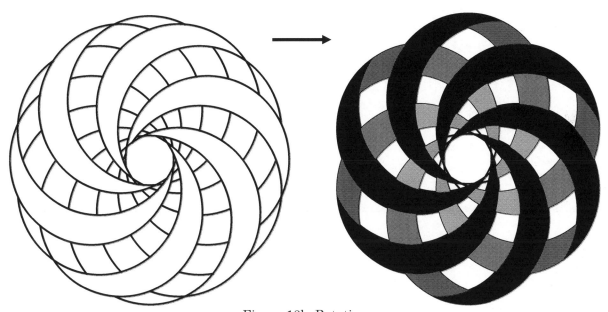

Figure 13b, Rotation.

In Figure 13a, we create circles on each of the vertices of the dodecagon, taking care that their size is determined by further vertices. As with everything we've done, the skeletal form itself is attractive. It's how we then proceed which determines what we will create this day. With one method of erasure we provide again for rotational movement. Shading can very much help one to see the "spherical" form which is created. Various shades of color must be imagined in place of the black, grey and white, which are presented here.

Finally, the next page; Figures 13c, show a variety of approaches we may take with the form from 13a. The last most presents the impression which any of these forms could make in a larger drawing (Figure 13d).

Figures 13c, A variety of projects.

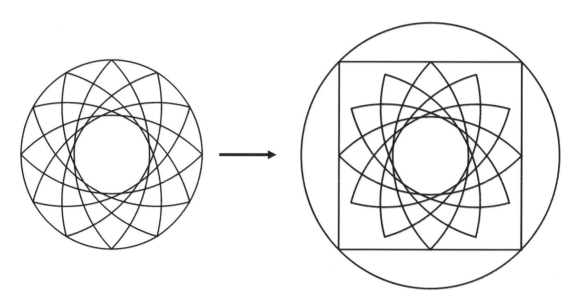

Figure 13d, Placing the image into the next higher scheme.

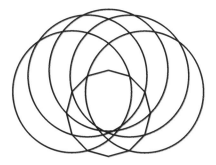

Figure 13e, Erasure provides a clamshell.

Ultimately, as the next diagrams show, further complexity can be achieved (always). Here, note that the outer bank of circles pass through the center of the dodecagon (meaning that their radii are smaller than in the previous group of drawings); basically two overlaying flower of life drawings, one rotated by a twelfth of the circle.

Figure 14a, The dodecagon and flower of life (2 each) conceptually joined.

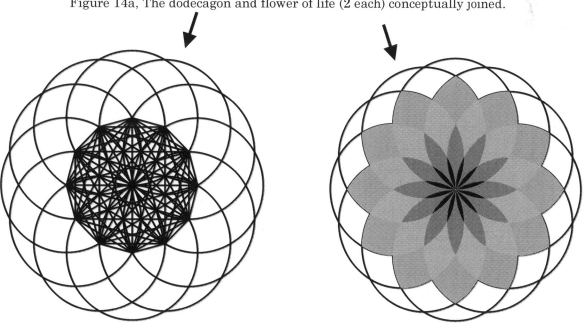

Figure 14b, Two possible creations of the mind.

Additional rings, whose circles are enlarged by the requirements of the drawing, are demonstrated on the next page. See the facets of the worked gem, the pupil of the eye.

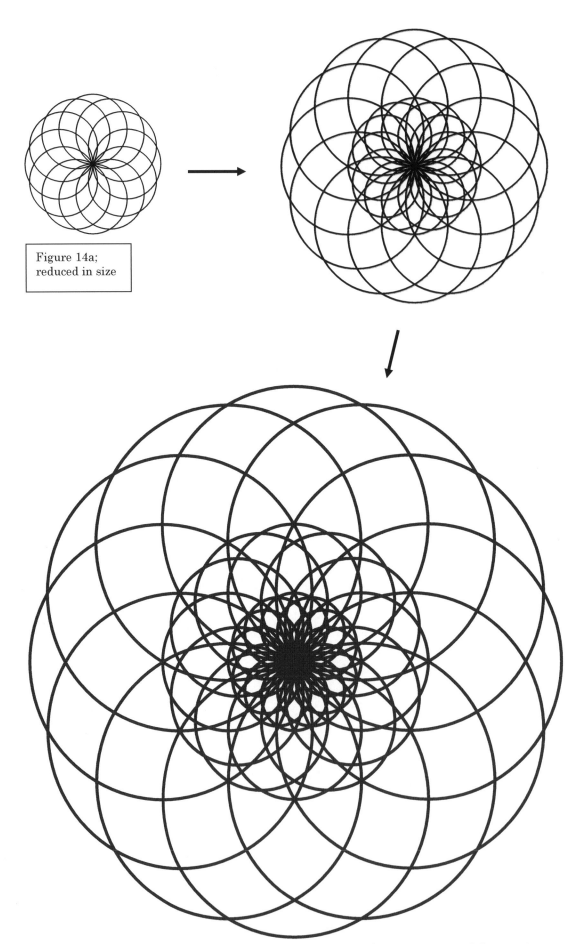

Figure 14a;
reduced in size

Figures 14c, Circles of ever increasing size, their centers at the extremities of the previous set.
(like electron cloud layers).

40

Our work evolves... One of the oldest religious traditions in ancient Egypt related to their Ogdoad of eight Gods, worshipped at Hermopolis. Here was the temple of Thoth; the self created One, lord of the Moon. The Ogdoad were four sets of male/female twins. Later forms of Egyptian religion changed the numbers and names; each larger city generally hosted its own set of Gods. At the site the Greeks would call after their own solar God – Heliopolis, the Egyptians worshipped nine Dieties; named the Ennead (like Enneagram).

Numbers are found in religious texts around the world, like 19 and 40. Perhaps some archetypal counting which is long since lost to us. We have so far worked a lot with three, four, six, and twelve. These have been seen to work very well together, visually, but also as far as measurement of the circle. Let us briefly look at numbers, in a context different from what we are used to.

**One**. What could this number represent symbolically? For many people today; one true God. It could also mean the Self. We can represent One with a dot on the paper or also show One with a circle. Remembering that ancient religions had the Sun as a major member of their pantheon (if not the main one – Ra), it is not surprising then that the astrological symbol for the sun is a circle with a point in it. A unit measure of one is the best term for use in understanding a wealth of mathematical relationships. One represents Me.

**Two** represents You and Me. Why is the yin and yang important in the East? Duality. This concept however is far from foreign in the West: Good/evil, light/dark, and Masculine/Feminine are commonly paired, perhaps going in opposite directions. Unfortunately, this is a tired paradigm. Could we not instead think in terms of tension, complementation, and cooperation? Many ancient religions believed in pairs. Plato's story of Atlantis mentions five sets of twin Gods (all male) who ruled the Atlantic. We are reminded of Gemini and Pisces. For the ancients, double numbers were common, such as 11/22 and 28/56 being used together. In math, with two points we may connect them and create a line.

**Three** points define a plane, a surface. It is the number of the mediator. Relationships. The Trinity, is a major tenet of Christianity; Father, Son, and the Holy Spirit. The main Gods of the Hindus are three; Vishnu, Siva, and Brahma. The Star of David, or Solomon's Seal, is not so much a six pointed star as it is two equilateral triangles in harmonic conjunction/opposition. That pointing upwards is called agni by the Indians; fire, masculine. The complementary is shakti; water, feminine. Their Auyrvedic system of health believes there are three types of body composition; water, air, and fire. They treat each accordingly when prescribing food and medicine. The alchemists of Europe used these two triangles to represent the same substances, with slight modifications to indicate air and earth.

Figure 1, Alchemical symbols of the first four elements.

What then does **four** represent? Mathematically we can think of one point above our three-point plane: volume – 3D space. The first Platonic form; the tetrahedron (*also* thought to represent fire), is a physical representation of this and is a key form in chemistry. Methane: $CH_4$, contains a central Carbon with the four Hydrogens finding a chemically balanced state according to tetrahedral geometry. Four, in nearly every culture is thought to represent key directions: NSEW, and reflects the corners of the home (except for those living in round domiciles). The zodiacal symbol of Earth; a circle with a cross in it represents this: matter.

**Five** is this Matter in motion; Life. It is a basic unit of counting. Our hand is its calculator. Five petals on a flower often indicates edibility: apple, rosehip, pear, peach, cherry, rasp–, black–, blue–, and strawberries, and plum. The Chinese system of health (alchemical in nature) uses five elements: earth, air, water, fire, and metal. Other cultures substitute for metal the concept of Æther. Plato, in describing the five regular forms related them thusly: fire – tetrahedron, air – octahedron, earth – cube, water – icosahedron, and cosmos – dodecahedron. The five-pointed star is a very ancient and mystical symbol, finding renewed use today. As we will see, this symbol does represent the Human, and is used ubiquitously: grades of rank, symbol of excellence, placed on flags, the Law. Cut open an apple across its axis, and peer inside to see the five-pointed star. Something to consider when we read that Eve took the apple from the tree of knowledge.

**Six**, is Time and Space. Six petals on flowers is nearly as common as five. This is a higher harmonic of three. We see that it is a building block of All of the geometry we have so far created. It is a building block of nature, as the bees show us in their hives. This is the structure of the snowflake, due to water's bipolar *and* "tetrahedral" nature. When we look to Solomon's Seal we see the six pointed star, duality, and if we look closely, that the star tetrahedron shares this geometry.

**Seven** defines sacred space: four directions plus up, down, and within. Electrons orbit the nucleus in a figure-eight pattern, on three axes; an octahedral structure denoting six directions, plus the center. Seven are the days in our week, and was revered by the ancient mystery schools, reflected in Catholicism's seven sacraments. Seven are the chakras (though some believe there are others – above and below the body, totaling twelve). The alchemists believed in seven base metals and associated seven known planets (including Sun and Moon) to them. While the five-pointed star is the first difficult construction, the seven-pointed is tantalizing and mystical. Why were there 7 wonders in the ancient world? Why is 7 considered lucky (with 11)? Seven were the rays upon the head of the Mithraic sun god, and also the statue of liberty, which bears a striking artistic resemblance.

Figure 2, Statue of Liberty (US gov.) and the Mithraic Solar diety (Francis Cumont 1912).

We touched already upon **eight** but let's include within this discussion the eight-fold path of Buddhism, 16ths of an inch, 8 divisions of the I Ching and the octagram, 64 divisions in the eye of Ra, 2 cups to a pint, 2 pints to a quart; 4 of which are in a gallon (16 cups): a gallon of water weighing 8 pounds, 64 positions on a chessboard; with 32 pieces, 16 pawns, 4 capitol pieces each color, and two pairs of royalty, and four suits in cards (tarot included), with four kings, queens, and jacks (there are four "personality" types in tarot – sixteen in total). Eastern – Western games of 64 and 16? Adults have 32 teeth. With the secondary directions, such as northwest, we have eight divisions of the circle. Hannukah lasts 8 days. Finally, the Taoists of China have beautiful myths of the 8 Immortals.

**Nine** is a number holy to many cultures. Chinese symbolism includes nine dragons, a creature whose energy is thought to be pervasive in the land, water and sky. Part of Taoism includes nine emperor Gods of prosperity and good health, who are celebrated in the first nine days of their ninth lunar month. Hindus celebrate nine days and nights at the start of Summer and Winter, beginning with 3 days of cleansing, three of spirit, and three of wisdom. Upon reaching enlightenment, Buddha had nine supreme attributes. The Maya had nine Lords/Ladies of the night; watching over rain, maize, youth, love... Many are interested in the "nine signs" of the Hopi, which indicate that the Fifth world is about to begin. Their religion also talks of nine universal kingdoms. The Greeks believed in the nine muses, and the Norse Odinic mysteries counted nine worlds. Many Mayan pyramids and Chinese pagodas had nine levels. We will see Magic with five, seven, and nine. We have much still to learn about nine.

While perhaps containing mystery of its own, **ten** is more about simplicity: it is our fingers put together. The top of the blossom holds five petals, while the reverse shows the five pointed star of the green bud casing after it has opened.

More interesting is **twelve**. There were twelve Gods (24 letters) in Greece and elsewhere. Christ had twelve apostles. Twelve is the number of edges in both the octahedron and cube. (Six is the similar count in the tetrahedron, and thirty in the remaining two forms). When we count edges, corners, and faces in the five basic forms, we generate 4, 6, 8, 12, 20, and 30. These are all critical values. More information on twelve is liberally spread throughout this book.

What of **twenty**, signally important to Mayan (and other) counting? The Maya had two counting systems of 13 x 20 and 18 x 20 days. The former is a number associated to Venus and is the approximate duration of nine moon cycles, and the period of Human gestation. The latter could roughly be associated with one year. Twenty of these was called a katun, a further twenty of which was a baktun of 144,000 (12x12x1000) days. It is the 13th of these which will end on the 12th of December in the year 2012, thus beginning the 14th great cycle. Twenty is a unique form of counting, with very ancient roots, predominantly found on both coastal regions of the Atlantic, and with isolated groups such as the Ainu, Albanians, and Georgians. It is half of forty, a number very common to Western religious tradition.

Finally, **thirty** is the approximate number of days in a month, twelve (plus a fraction) of which equates to one solar cycle or year. Thirty and twelve count very well together in our 360 based measurement system, just as their "twins" of 24 and 60 work so well for timekeeping. Thirty, twenty, twelve, eight. All are significant to the science and intelligence behind mathematics; as are many, if not all, of these others.

Sacred Number is a key ingredient to Sacred Geometry.

"There appeared a great wonder in Heaven; a woman clothed with the sun, and the moon under her feet, and upon her head a crown of twelve stars... and behold a great red dragon, having seven heads and ten horns, and seven crowns upon his heads... the seven heads are seven mountains... and there are seven kings...and I heard a great voice out of the temple, saying to the seven angels..." – Revelations:12 – 17.

**Eight**

We now return to the circle, placing a top mark upon it and using the compass to find two more marks. Using symmetry now (as we should have been able to do even earlier), we find the bottom point. We will bisect the two side marks (drawing arcs from each and connecting across their intersections).

In Figure 3a we used the same daisy geometry as presented in Chapter One, but really the compass has to only be visually more than half the distance between the two side marks and the intercepts will still provide the bisection. With symmetry we obtain the diamond, which shows a square when rotated by 45°.

In Figure 3b, we will again seek a bisection (here the compass was adjusted to be *visually* more than half of the side needing to be divided by two). The bisection lines, and the resulting square they help to generate are then given in Figure 3c.

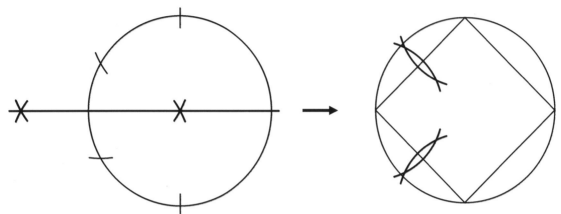

Figure 3a, Construction points and lines          Figure 3b, Four fold division and side bisection.

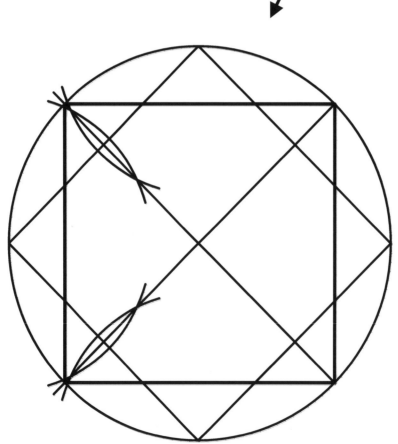

Figure 3c, Two squares, forming eight – fold division.

Once the preliminary sketchwork is complete, we may resume our play!

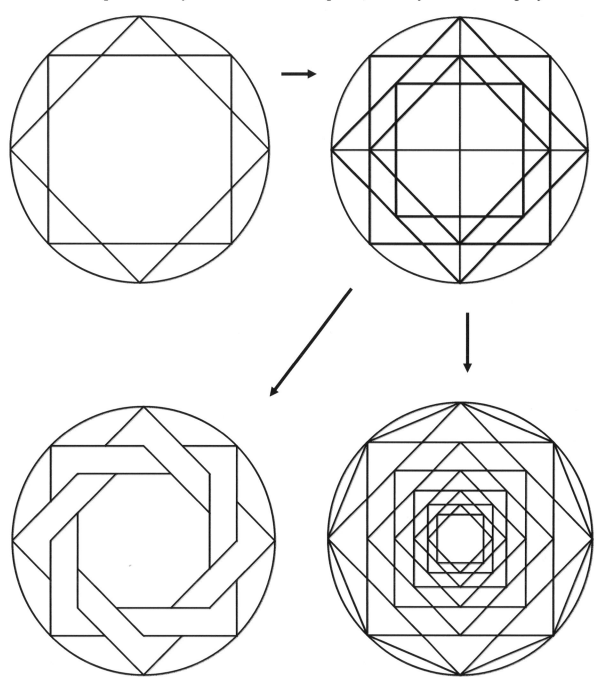

Figures 4, Various forms created from eight – fold division, each step proportional by √2.

The work so far has only proceeded a small amount from that which we've done prior. But, eight – fold is a great step away from 3–, 6–, and 12– fold. Ancient megalithic cultures of Europe held a 16 – month calendar. The sixteen based counting retained in Great Britain is reminiscent of this, as are the eight Pagan holy days of the two solstices, two equinoxes and four other important holidays.

We will see that 3–, 6–, and 12– fold division are fundamental to trigonometry and Sacred Geometry, but that 16– fold intersects them; part of (while not part of) their system.

We will proceed further, using the intercepts of the square and diamond thus far achieved to provide for an additional eight points (Figure 5).

We now have sixteen equally spaced points around the circle and from this we may generate an octagon aligned parallel to the edges of the page.

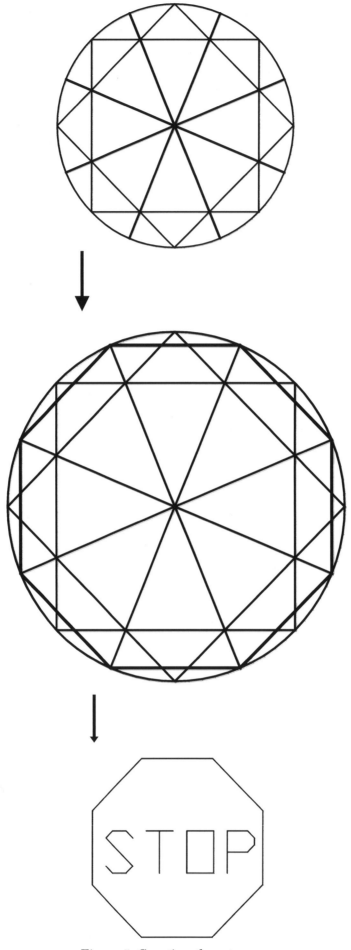

Figure 5, Creating the octagon.

Octagonal work brings to a close the "easy" projects which we can do in our study of Sacred Geometry, which to now has mostly been a study in Mandala. The key has been that we open our selves and mind as we get acquainted with the compass, play with idea and color, and read at least a little about number. Let's work a bit now with the octagon, in ways similar and also different.

From the octagon, extend four lines outward from its center exactly double the center-to-edge midpoint distance, as shown in Figure 6. From there draw four more circles of the same size as the original, on the cardinal directions. Use these to trim specific lines to obtain the Maltese cross.

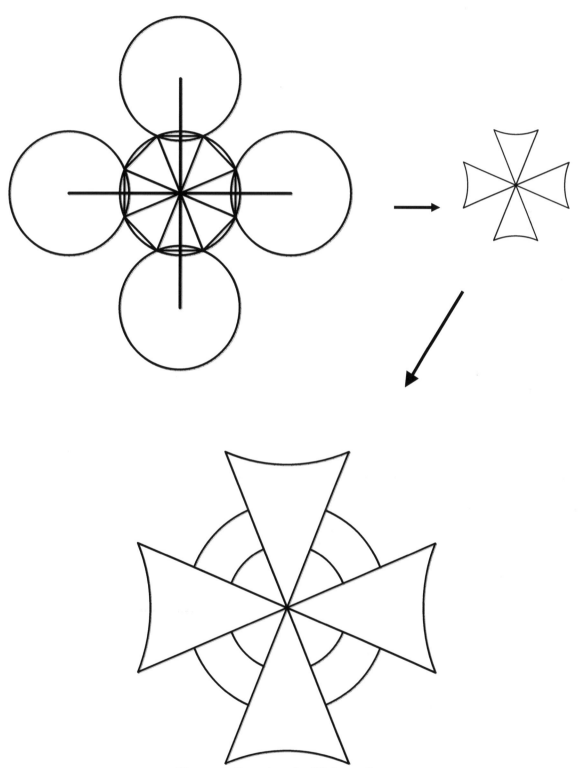

Figure 6, Creating the Maltese Cross

As an alternative, let's use the sixteen points, drawing a square through each fourth point (four squares in total). The first image in Figure 7a demonstrates this. Beside it we see two octagons wrapped around these squares, making a rather elegant figure. Or, draw additional squares inside these first four, taking the image inward, as we have done so many times already with other numeric patterns.

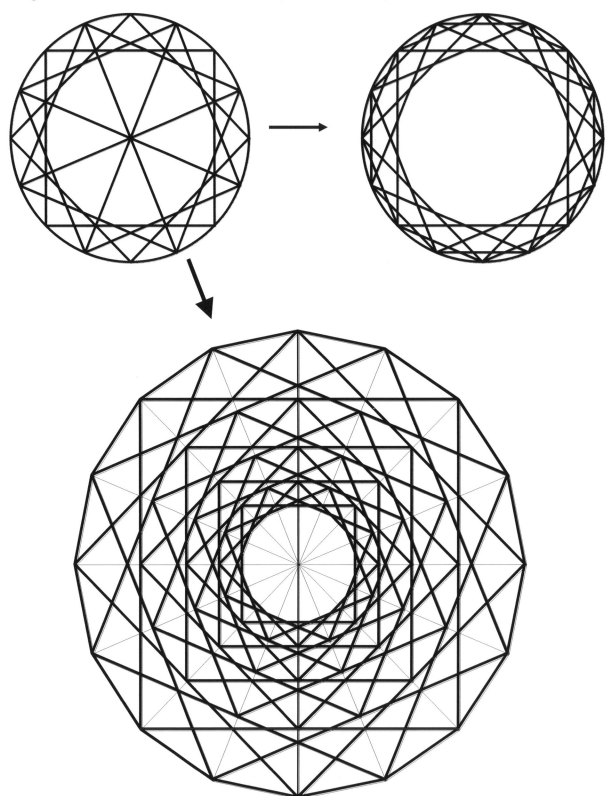

Figure 7a, Creating a spider web for 16 − fold, using squares.

As usual, we may then proceed to erase, fill, and color this image in the variety of ways portrayed in Figures 7b, with or without lines.

Figure 7b, Shading techniques for the 16 – fold web.

49

There is more work (play) which can be performed with eight – fold geometry. One pleasant form, is shown in Figure 8. This star can easily be colored green and red for a seasonal effect. A more elaborate scheme is also provided.

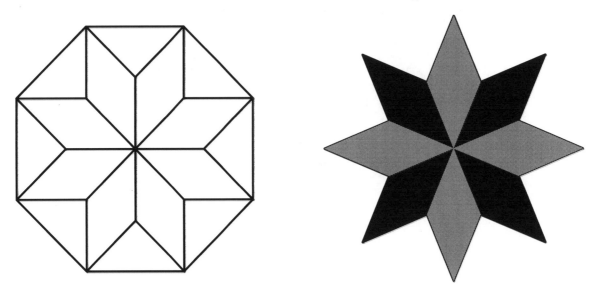

Figure 8a, A different kind of star.

Figure 8b, Something more.

Figure 9, Islamic pattern

In Figure 9 we have another route of exploration with eight. This pattern has been very beautifully used in Islamic art, and is quite symbolic. We can think of each black "X" as a contraction from a square, while the white diamond is an expansion. Breathing in and out; complementation.

Eight – fold geometry can be found in nature; a great representation being spiders, with eight legs and two body sections (insects are 6 – fold, with six legs and three body sections). Four petalled flowers are also quite common.

Many ancient cultures believed in eight winds, each a harbinger of different weather. This can be represented in two ways, as Figure 10 shows. The images show the Greek Platonic and Pythagorean philosophy of four elements, interspersed with four qualities.

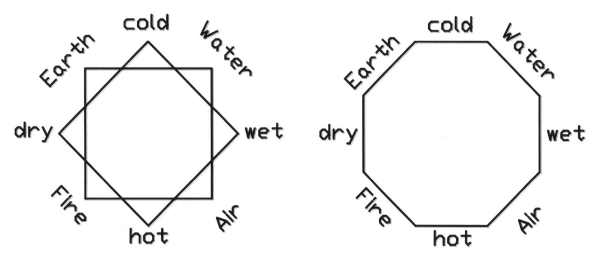

Figure 10, Four elements, and between each a unique effect.

Symbolism can know many forms. Archetypal counts can be found throughout history in the form of 8 and 12.

## Sacred symbols

We have been thus far approaching Sacred Geometry visually, and through numeric philosophy. Now that we know something about working with the compass, let's create symbols used by various religions and cultures around the world. We will delve into these symbols at least some little bit, as we attempt to further understand the Sacredness of Geometry.

Probably the easiest to make is the Qabbalah. This word has many variant spellings, such as Kabbalah and Cabala. Interesting are the three syllables: Ka, Ba, and La. The former two were important terms in the Egyptian religion. Ka was the "seat of the Soul", while "Ba", was the Spirit. This is a concept still alive today as Astrologers say that Moon represents the Soul; that person's essence which has been born again and again, while Sun represents the Spirit; or what the Being wishes to do in *this* life. We see these same syllables used in the naming of the Islamic holy of holies; the Ka'aba. We will soon see further examples.

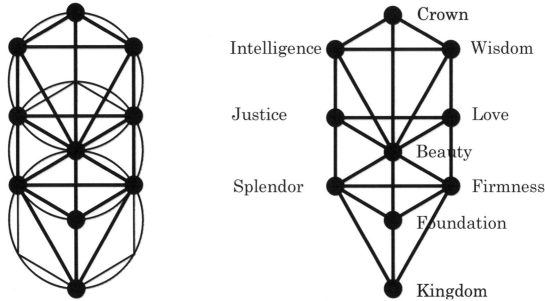

Figure 11, Qabbalah.

The Qabbalah is readily created from our original daisy (Figure 11). But what *is* Qabbalah? In the holy book called the Sepher Yezirah, it is said that "By thirty two paths of secret wisdom, the Eternal, the Lord of Hosts, the God of Israel the living God, the King of the Universe, the Merciful and Gracious, the High and Exalted God, He who inhabits Eternity, Glorious and Holy is His name, hath created the world by means of number, word, and writing, (or number, numberer, and numbered)." This book is considered one of the first philosophical books written in Hebrew. Scholars are not clear when it was written but perhaps from around 700 AD. It and the Qabbalah may originate from the Jewish mystical community in Spain, or from far earlier and elsewhere. The first clear use of Qabbalah seems to be recorded around 1350.

Referring to the figure we see that there are ten "nodes", called Sephira (sphere); Sephiroth as a plural form. These are considered as emanations of En Soph; the infinite governor of the world. These emanations can be thought of as active and passive, feminine and masculine. The top three are associated with the world of thought (spirit). The middle three are considered to be with the world of the soul and the final four are linked with the world of the body.

It can be counted that there are 22 "paths" which connect the sephiroth. These are linked to the 22 letters of the Hebrew alphabet. The Jewish mystics were very much into Gematria; the relation of letter to number. Our A; their aleph, represented the number '1', beth (hence aleph-beth; the precursor of our alphabet) was counted as '2', and so forth. So, written words could be summed up as specific numbers and thus certain numbers became very holy. The Greeks continued this practice, and so for example the Grecian spelling of the word Holy Spirit totaled 1080; which is 3 x 360...

Twenty-two is the number of personality cards in the Tarot. It has been said that to truly become a "Metaphysicist", one must study Qabbalah, Tarot, Magic, and Alchemy. All four of these "Sciences" were at their height at the close of the Renaissance.

Twenty-two is further broken down into the three parent letters: aleph, mem, and shin; seven "double" numbers and twelve so-called simple consonants. One beautiful representation of this, also called Sepher Yetzirah, is shown in Figure 12. Beside it is an alchemical drawing. Notice the use of astrological symbols there-in. These represented the seven metals associated with each "planet". See not only the 7-pointed star but also an underlying equilateral triangle.

As with Mandala, these forms are meant for meditation. To the mystic, learning and using Qabbalah is a long process of development.

Figure 12 Sephir Yetzirah and alchemical artwork (L'Azoth des Philosophes Basil Valentine, Paris, 1659).

Shifting our focus now, we will generate a set of circles as shown in Figure 13 (based on the vesica piscis), seeing that we can easily create the Christian cross, in its "Latin" and much earlier Greek form (known to predate the birth of Christianity by several centuries). This brings home to us an interesting concept that much of which we find in the scriptures of various religions carries messages and ideas from much earlier text and religious traditions. Christianity itself has for example several feast days which are Pagan in origin, such as Easter being the Germanic rebirth of Spring, and the birth of Jesus being associated with December 25th is coincident with the earlier Mithraic belief that the sun god – Sol Invicti (sun victorious) was reborn each year at this time. Frankincense and Myrrh were ritual incenses used in Egyptian temple science.

We take for granted many symbols today, and often seek differences. But as with the golden rule, several beliefs are shared by most all, and their symbols are perhaps much more complex then they appear.

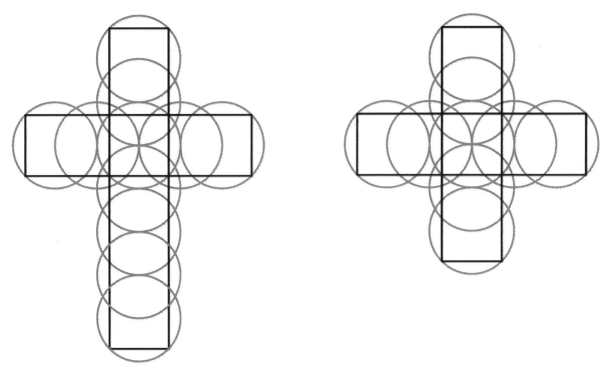

Figure 10, Latin and Greek crosses generated by a series of circles.

A really interesting and challenging symbol to create in mandalic work is the Tibetan infinity symbol. For this, we need to start with a diamond shape. We need to divide each edge into thirds; called trisecting. We could instead measure, requiring a side length to the diamond which is easily divisible by '9' (for this we need a circle radius which is some multiple of approximately '6.363', or roughly 6 and 3/8 (some of the math for this will be explained shortly). Or, we can employ a Euclidean technique; with the compass (Figure 14)!

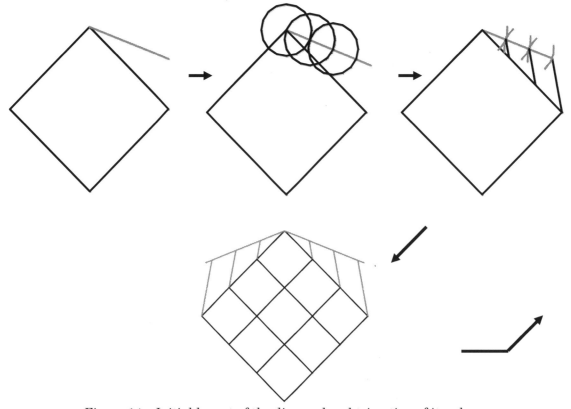

Figure 14a, Initial layout of the diamond and trisection of its edges.

54

To begin, we draw a new line from one of the points of the diamond, and then three circles as shown in Figure 14a. Really, we only need arcs; to mark three equally spaced segments on this new line. From the end of the rightmost segment, draw a line to the end of the diamond. Two lines drawn parallel to this denote the other thirds of this edge. Repeat for the opposite side.

We then echo this process to further trisect each of the boxes so far created. This is shown in Figure 14b. (image shown enlarged)

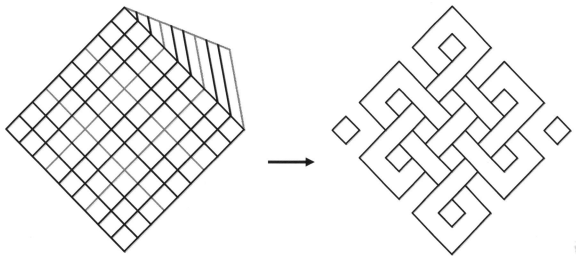

Figure 14b, Division of the sides into 9 equal segments and then erasure to achieve the result.

Now just a *little* erasure and we obtain the infinity symbol, enjoying the weave pattern. We can enclose this within a circle, within a square; two forms that are the basis for many concepts in Sacred Geometry. If we rotate this image by 45° we do in fact see that it is in the form of a square.

Figure 14c, The final product.

A further Sacred Geometry symbol is called the Bagua, from Chinese and Taoist tradition. It is presented, along with some steps to create it, in Figure 12. This symbol is used with Feng Shui and other processes of prediction. There are 64 (8 x 8) "trigrams" associated with it and also connections to the holy book – the I Ching. More specific detail will be given on the yin and yang in the next chapter.

Figure 15a, Start with twelve little circles and a vertical line.

Figure 15b, Octagonal Taoist symbol from the I Ching.

We are coming to the end of our introduction to Sacred Geometry, which has mostly been a rigorous effort in drawing various "mandalas", or geometric patterns in the round. As the word Mandala comes from the East, we will look to try and better define it with the diagram in Figure 16. The process of creating a Mandala is meditational, as we think, work, erase, and color. We can spend time at this, and then more time sitting back and enjoying the work, or gazing upon it with more intent. As we go from the "basic" ideas presented in this book, we can think that not only colors and lines can present our thoughts and feelings, but that we can intentionally place objects within the picture to give it even more meaning.

Too, at some point we need to let go of rigid form and while maintaining some uniformity, perhaps our drawings can include some items done in free-hand.

56

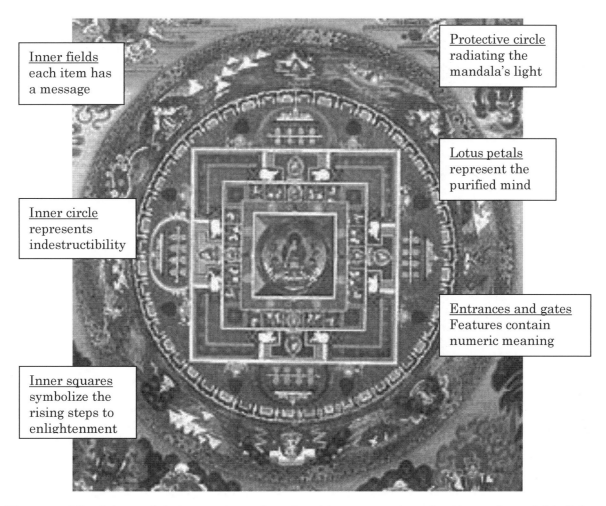

Inner fields
each item has
a message

Protective circle
radiating the
mandala's light

Inner circle
represents
indestructibility

Lotus petals
represent the
purified mind

Inner squares
symbolize the
rising steps to
enlightenment

Entrances and gates
Features contain
numeric meaning

Figure 16, Mandalas and their meanings.  Imagine this as a top view of a 3D temple model (wiki).

"Mandalas" it has been said are used by every culture, as the following examples will show.  Nor are they limited to two dimensions.  Notice in Figure 17 an aerial view layout of Borobudor, and a near top-down view.  We see a mandala, rising in steps toward the center, (and a lot of use of 5, 6, and 7).  In later figures we are shown a dream catcher, celtic knot, and a rose window from Chartres cathedral.  Note especially in this latter (Figure 18), that various symbols are buried within the whole.

In Figure 19 we see a typical gothic portal (Chartres) and a unique tower found guarding a similar portal (Ulm).  Allegory to human genitalia (thus inclusion of feminine and masculine in the artwork) is obvious.  A joining of male and female is also accomplished in Bernini's St. Peter's Basilica and palazzia (Figure 20).

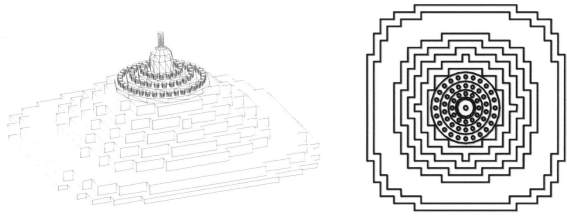

Figure 17, Borobudor, two views.

Figure 18, Rose window from Chartres cathedral

Figure 19, Portal from Chartres and tower from Ulm (Wikipedia), showing female/male.

Figure 20, Dream Catcher, Celtic knot (wikipedia), Male-female in the holiest of places; Rome.

A further unique form of mandala is the yantra, or sri yantra. A modern example is provided in Figure 21. Many times, people who gaze upon mandalas in meditation (or also upon a point in space), will chant, rhythmically reciting what is called a mantra. Reflection and meditation are meant to free the mind. The sound vibration is thought to represent a spiritual concept. Similarly, a yantra is a visual vibration of a spiritual concept.

Many times we see lotus petals ringing the drawing. These can be found around many diagrams, and are associated with those representing the chakras. According to Steiner, we must reflect on these petals to get them in motion, through specific exercises, so that we may see higher worlds and Beings.

Figure 21, Expanded Sri Yantra (by Francene Hart) and also the 7 chakras, with their lotus petals.

59

Figure 22, "Celtic" knot – (Leonardo da Vinci)

We've come far in our studies. The adept is now left to face the challenge presented by Figure 22. Notice the count of 16. We will return to this number as we conclude this chapter. While we today use a twelve and 360 based calendar and counting system, and 12 and 16 based measuring system still in many English speaking countries, early inhabitants of those British Isles are thought to have kept not a twelve but a 16 month calendar. A calendar wheel is presented in conclusion, so that the reader may see dates which we still note Today with various rituals so named, or changed (All soul's day, the Assumption, etc.) depending on one's Faith. Eight-fold symbolic geometry can be found elsewhere.

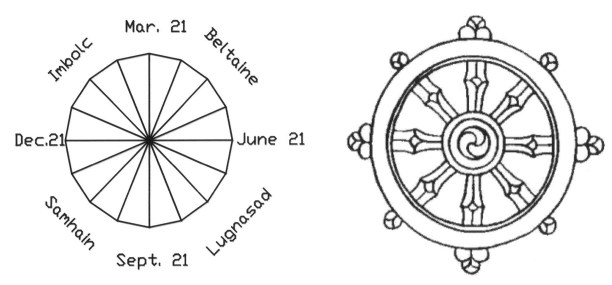

Figure 23, Pagan calendar derived from ancient megalithic

Figure 24, Dharma wheel, from the Indian subcontinent (wiki)

# Fourth Chapter – 3D

Sacred Geometry is not only a two dimensional proposition. We saw at the end of the last chapter that an overhead view of architecture (especially sacred) can appear as a flat mandala. Conversely, there are many times when we may represent something in 2D such that it appears to be three-dimensional. Too, if we aren't careful, we might mistake something which is 3D for two, depending upon our perspective.

Were we to play with our original drawing process of 6 equally spaced points around the circle, we could obtain any one of the images shown in Figure 1.

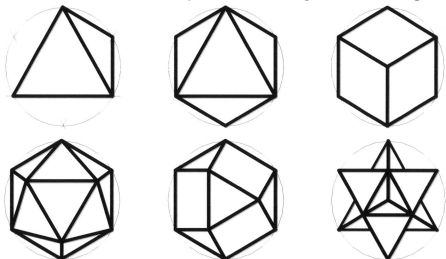

Figure 1, Various "3D" forms generated by six – fold division.

In Figure 1 we see a familiar form; the cube. To its left is an 8-sided diamond, which is the shape that natural diamonds come in (also fluorite and other crystals). As was earlier mentioned, this is also a normal atomic structure. Further, salt and other compounds have a cubic crystalline structure. We see both of these and two more of the five Platonic forms. Then comes one of the thirteen Archimedic forms, which Archimedes discovered by variously trimming the edges off of those of his predecessor. All of these are "regular", meaning the edge lengths are equal.

The sixth diagram presents two interwoven tetrahedrons, called the star tetrahedron. Many people Today call this the Merkaba. Some meditate with these, imagining themselves seated inside one; the upward pointing tetrahedron; fire, spinning counterclockwise (Earthwise), sending energy upward, and the downward pointing form; water, spinning clockwise (Sunwise). This term Merkaba was the name given to the chariot or four-wheeled vehicle driven by the Cherubim in Ezekiel's vision. We may notice again the syllables ka and ba. Interestingly, "mer" is found in the mythical Mt. Meru of the Hindu, the Staff of Meru, or spine; the bridge between cosmos and earth, and also the Egyptian name for their pyramids; mr. Similarities of culture identify mer, mr, as a place of ascension.

Note that the fourth image, the icosahedron, needs a little "adjustment" to that central triangle to get the image to appear just right. This is reflected in the artwork on the cover. Still, the hexagon is instrumental in creating the overall form, just as it has historically been used by artists (Figure 2).

It is interesting that 2D can look like 3D and vice – versa. Notice too in Figures 4 and 5 how the images appear to contain a Star of David, when held appropriately. Thus, the 6–pointed star is even more interesting, as it can be a variety of unique three-dimensional objects projected or viewed in two.

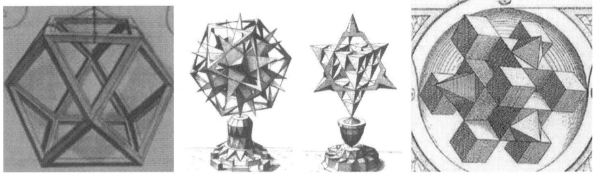

Figure 2, 2D – 3D Geometries by da Vinci and Jamnitzer

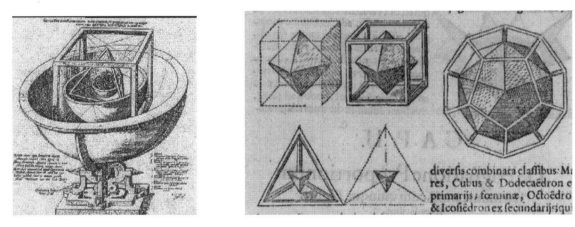

Figure 3, Platonic artwork by Kepler. The left-most is a fairly accurate model of our solar system.

Figure 4, The icosa – and dodecahedrons. Wire framed 3D forms in a 2D photo.

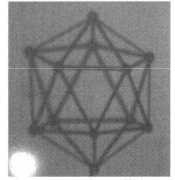

Figure 5, Shadow cast on the wall through an Icosahedron.

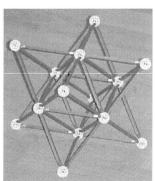

The Merkaba, off – axis.

We want to play with these images, drawing, letting our imagination dance. And then, we want to construct them for real.

A fun exercise to do is to draw a hexagon per our usual techniques. In fact, do four of them. Three should be exactly half the size of the last, for example using radii of 2" and then 4". Draw radial lines across the drawings. Now, cut the hexagons out of the paper, along their external edges. Fold them once along each of the three axial lines. Finally, cut along one of those lines in toward the center. It will be seen now that the paper wants to "turn", to become three-dimensional. We can in fact rotate then once, twice, and finally three times, obtaining each of the pictures shown in Figure 6b.

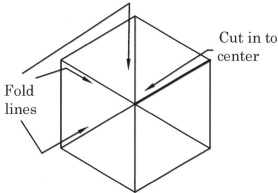

Figure 6a, Cut out, fold (each of 3 axis) and make an incision.

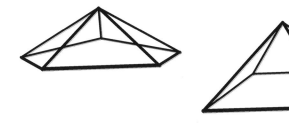

Figure 6b, Rotating our paper-fold creates these "pyramidal" structures.

The three fold-up pyramids are parts of three different Platonic forms. The tetrahedron is easy. If we take two of our smaller pyramids, each folded to have a four sided base, and flip one up-side-down, we see that they could go together, making a diamond shape, as shown in the center of Figure 6c. If all four pyramids had a 3-sided base, and were placed the smaller three around the larger, they'd make the beginnings of the star tetrahedron. Finally, take the three smaller pyramids and open each as a five-sided pyramid, laying these partially overlapping (one partly inside each other). This will show the beginning of the icosahedron.

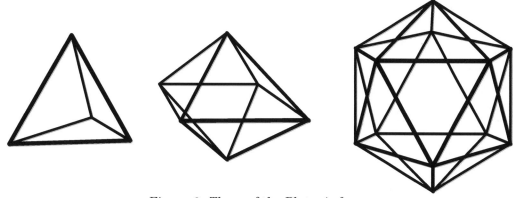

Figure 6c Three of the Platonic forms

Flat layouts for making tetra–, octa–, and icosahedrons are given in Figure 7. Constructions steps are as follows: Select a firmer grade of paper, draw the desired layout (using the daisy drawing techniques – with additional circles), and color a pattern on this, cutout, fold, glue a string inside (for hanging) and then glue together (leave tabs for this).

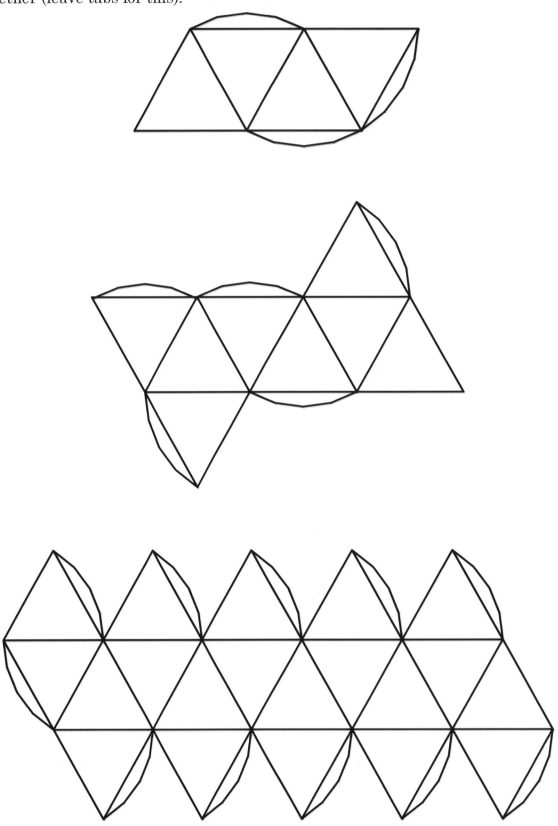

Figure 7, Patterns for making the Tetra–, Octa–, and Icosahedron.

We began with Platonic forms having equilateral triangles as their faces because this is in keeping with the flow of work we performed at the start of this book, and for their ease and interesting process in construction. We will now make the cube. To begin, we need to draw a cross (using now octagonal techniques), cut it out (keeping tabs), and then fold and glue together.

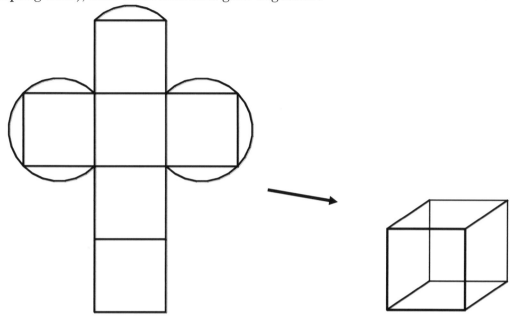

Figure 8, Creating the cube from a flat pattern.

Now that we have four of the Platonic forms constructed, we can begin to "decipher" them, needing this cube for our beginning. This study will be scientific, mathematical. For this we need a tool known as the Pythagorean theorem. It is hoped that not only will the reader *not* despair, but that they will begin to finally understand their possibly tortuous high school mathematics experience.

Pythagoras was one of the earliest of "Renaissance" men, having actually lived about 20 centuries earlier! Raised and educated in Greece, he went on to study (and probably be initiated in) Egyptian temple science, followed by further travels and studies in Babylon; the then heir to Sumerian knowledge. From this long exile he returned to Grecian climes; actually a colony in southern Italy. He formed a school here and was sought out by those who wanted his knowledge, philosophy, and wisdom. His educational goals went beyond his school and into society at large, which he wanted to reform and refine. Upon his death at a late age (though still perhaps not from natural causes), his school was closed, his students hunted, and most of his written records destroyed. Much of what we know about him has been recorded by others, most of whom were far from contemporaries.

Pythagoras is credited with a theorem which was certainly known far earlier to the Egyptians. They used a rope with twelve equally spaced knots to create right angles in their fields each year after the flooding of the Nile. If one were to hold the third and then seventh knots, with the help of a friend, the remaining 5–segment portion of the rope could be brought around to make a right triangle.

We know this theorem according to $a^2 + b^2 = c^2$, where a and b are short sides in a right triangle (having a 90° angle) and c is the adjoining long side. We may literally say "the square on each of the short sides, added together equals the square on the longest side". We will demonstrate this but first let's look at a table of select "squared" values (Table 1). Try to find patterns in the squared values of the first thirteen numbers.

| 1 | 2 | 3 | 4 | 5 | 6 | 7 | 8 | 9 | 10 | 11 | 12 | 13 | 24 | 25 | 40 | 41 |
|---|---|---|---|---|---|---|---|---|----|----|----|----|----|----|----|----|
| 1 | 4 | 9 | 16 | 25 | 36 | 49 | 64 | 81 | 100 | 121 | 144 | 169 | 576 | 625 | 1600 | 1681 |

Table 1, Squared values of various numbers.

When one looks at Table 1, they hopefully see that a pattern develops between the squared values. The difference of the first two is '3', and of the next pair is '5', then '7', and so on. The difference of the fourth pair; 16 and 25 is 9, which is also the sum of the roots; 4 and 5. If we look further, we might notice that the difference between any two adjacent square values is the sum of the two base numbers which we begin with. This is a handy way of doing square values. For example 40 "squared" is simply 1600, and thus 41 squared is 1600 + 40 + 41 = 1681. Too, 40 + 41 is 81, which itself is a perfect square of the number 9.

Right triangles whose solutions are perfect numerical values are known as Pythagorean triangles. The easiest measures 3 x 4 x 5, which we see with the theorem visually demonstrated in Figure 9.

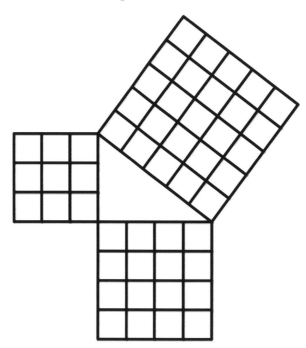

Figure 9, The squares drawn on the shortest possible sides; 3 and 4, and their outcome.

As was noted, 4 and 5 make 9, which is the short side of '3' squared. The next odd number, squared; 5 – 25, is the sum of 12 and 13; adjacent numbers. The next, 7 – 49, is the sum of 24 and 25. What this means is that while 3 x 4 x 5 is the first Pythagorean triangle, the next are 5 x 12 x 13, and 7 x 24 x 25, indicating that 9 and then 11 will be the short sides in the next triangles.

The numbers 3, 4, and 5 are an interesting combination. If we have six or more lines coming into a point, as we saw in our hexagon, we are restricted to a flat intersection; two-dimensional. But, as we saw with our fold-up of the hexagon cutout five lines coming together enables us to build the icosahedron. Four intersecting lines allows for the octahedron, and three lines at a given point is in the construction of the tetrahedron, cube, and yet to be introduced dodecahedron. Two lines at a node is but a corner of a flat plane. Too, the five platonic forms have faces that are triangular (3), square (4) and pentagonal (5).

Finally, the sum of 3, 4, and 5 is 12 and the three multiplied together is 60: not just random numbers but fundamental. The sum of 5, 12, and 13 is 30...

Something of interest in these Pythagorean triangles is that given their slopes: 3/4, 5/12, 7/24, and so forth, the slopes of the lines which bisect them (meaning that their angles measure half), will have slopes of 1/3, 1/5, 1/7,...while the bisectors of the reciprocals; 4/3, 12/5, 24/7,... have slopes of 1/2, 2/3, 3/4,... respectively. Such number combinations, of "clean" fractional gradients only work when consisting of perfect Pythagorean ratios. This is a special harmonic (Figure 10).

Something else of interest in the Pythagorean theorem is its "Logic". Note that such numbers as 2 and 3 total 5. But, in a right triangle of lengths 2 and 3, their longest side will measure √13. Conversely, √2 and √3 do not add up to make √5. But, they *do* "add up" in the right triangle, where √2 x √3 x √5, √3 x √4 x √7, etc. are real possibilities.

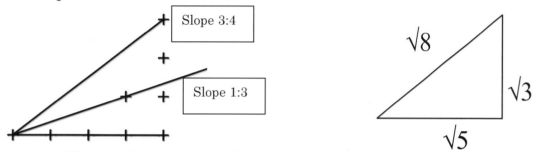

Figure 10, Demonstration of two gradients, one double the angle of the other.

Figure 11, Demonstration of the unique "additive" nature of the Pythagorean theorem.

Part of what makes Geometry Sacred is numeric facts such as these, and then their incorporation in Human physical and mental construction. One such construct is the cube. Hold the cube that has been made. On any given face, what is the longest length? The diagonal. Within the cube itself, what is the longest length? It is easier to view this with a skeletal or wire-framed cube; as afforded by such products as Zometools, Astro-logix, Tubespace, or Geo-mag. What is nice about the latter in particular is that it demonstrates the strength or stability of the various forms (the cube being among the weaker).

Using the Pythagorean theorem, and assuming an edge length of '1', the afore-mentioned lengths are rigidly held to values of √2 and √3, forming also a right triangle.

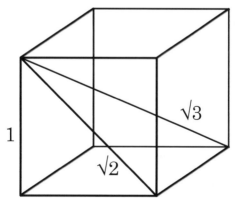

Figure 12, Unique lengths found in the cube.

These values are easy to obtain in the cube. In the octahedron, we can see that the longest length goes from top to bottom. How to calculate this using the Pythagorean theorem, if it is even possible? If we rotate the object in our hand, we see the square base contained within it. Not only are all diagonals (3 of them) equal, but they are √2; when the edge length is '1'! Again, not random, and interestingly the same value found in the cube.

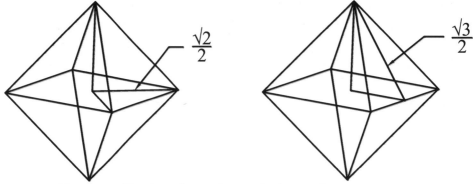

Figure 13, Key lengths in the octahedron (edges measure '1').

The tetrahedron requires a bit more effort. In the tetrahedron the longest length is the edge. An interesting thing to consider in these forms, as Plato viewed them, is how they best fill the sphere which encompasses them. Being regular means that they share centers with the sphere that could be defined by all of the vertexes. Plato's analysis of the five forms went in sequence based upon how they filled their sphere, with the tetrahedron being the least and the dodecahedron the most. This is perhaps why he assigned the forms each to an element, leaving the dodecahedron as the last, representing the cosmos. Tetrahedron symbolized fire, octahedron – air, cube – earth, and icosahedron – water. The triangle he described as the strongest of structures, and due to its construction, the tetrahedron the strongest of forms. This is a fact which Buckminster Fuller grasped and put into his work.

We can look inside the tetrahedron, using clues found in Figure 13 with the eight-faced form. How would we find the center (Figure 14a)? How would we find the specific lengths shown in Figure 14b? We have a little help for this. As the faces consist of equilateral triangles, we can use the specific length of √3/2; and an edge length of '1'. But more importantly, it just so happens that the tetrahedron defines half of the vertexes in a cube which could encompass it (Figure 14c).

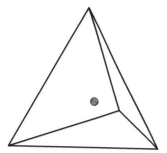

Figure 14a, Internal geometries of the tetrahedron.

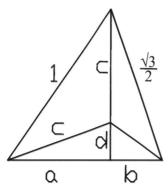

Figure 14b, key lengths.

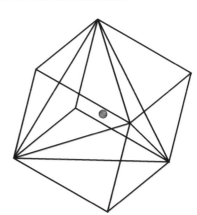

14c, A big help

68

Mathematics has had an inexorable march through the pages of history. We teach advanced mathematics Today, from algebra through geometry and trig, up to calculus, in a matter of a few brief years; often force-feeding a watered-down form to disinterested youth what was once the play of philosophers. But, the development took millennia, culminating in calculus only a few centuries ago. The ancients studied four areas when they looked at mathematics: number, the earth, the "stars", and music. They looked at number philosophically. They developed a word derived from the name for Earth: Gaia, the mother goddess, and metrion – "to measure" (geo-metry). The planets they poetically called stars and to calculate their movements they needed to triangulate, meaning trigonometry.

What is interesting is that they also looked to music. They believed in something called the "music of the spheres"; that each planet had its own song, vibration, or rhythm. All danced in universal harmony. Back on Earth, they found music to be very mathematical. Pieces of metal, having different sizes but the same consistency and form (bells) create different tones when struck, just as does a child's xylophone. Glasses of water do the same thing, when containing different volumes. String length in a harp or other instrument also determines tone, each of which is rigidly fixed by specific lengths; harmonious with other notes as determined by their proportions, particularly 1:2, 2:3 – the "fifth", and 3:4 – the "fourth". Finally, notes do not have to be of equal duration, but are stepped in time. Today, we call these whole, half, and quarter notes.

Looking to Figure 14d, we see some of this harmony (extensive calculation omitted). Our old friends are back; $\sqrt{2}$ and $\sqrt{3}$ (note that $\sqrt{6}$ is *just* $\sqrt{3} \times \sqrt{2}$). The fractions are different, though their common divisor is 12!

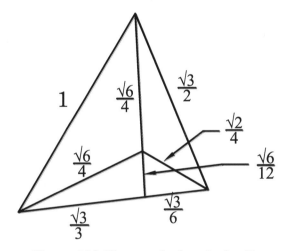

Figure 14d, The tetrahedron "solved".

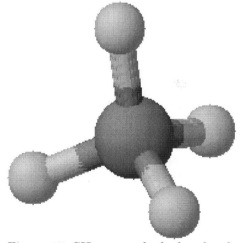

Figure 15, CH₄, a tetrahedral molecule

Our last thought on this form, at least in its "singular status", is to discuss the angles. From the center of the tetrahedron, when one node is aligned to north, the other three points are at what would be 19.5° below the "equator" determined by the center. This seems almost to be an angle of cosmic stress, as the volcanic Hawaiian islands are at this latitude, as is the largest volcano in our solar system; Olympus mons (Mars), plus the great red spot on Jupiter and the blue spot on Neptune. Too, it is the angle in which balanced molecules, such as methane, form themselves (Figure 15).

There are further geometric forms to explore. But lest we think that this is all about mathematics and calculation (most of which has been pared from this volume), we will look at Figure 16 to see that even Pythagorean triangles can be used as bases for mandala.

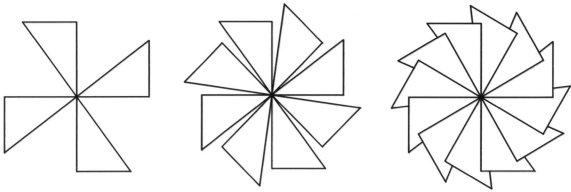

Figure 16, Fun with the 3–4–5 triangle.

In the first chapter, we briefly alluded to a form called the vesica piscis. We will use this item in more detail in the latter part of this book. Let's analyze it a bit now. The object consists of two circles drawn side-by-side, with centers being opposite equatorial edges. Figure 17a shows the left circle with the specific marks needed (generated with the compass) to then draw the right circle, "reverse engineering", to then get top and bottom points for it. We see then specific right triangles, which we will use to calculate the three lengths, in Figure 17b.

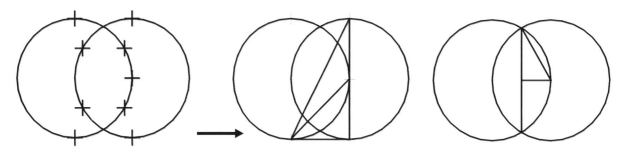

Figure 17a, Vesica piscis, with an eye towards specific geometries.

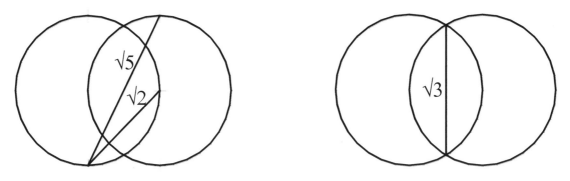

Figure 17b, Solution of those geometries.

This is yet another geometric expression of √2 and √3, with introduction of √5, which will become increasingly important to us. The Vesica piscis has been used throughout the middle ages in cathedral construction. Does application in Sacred Architecture denote Sacred Geometry? This form has also been discovered in a distant nebula, by the Hubble telescope.

We saw within the octahedron the special length of √3/2, which we then assumed within the tetrahedron (Figures 13 and 14). This is found in the equilateral triangle, as shown in Figure 18a, assuming as always an edge length of '1'. If we assume a radial length of '1', we also find it repeating itself in specific lengths as determined within our hexagon (Figure 18b).

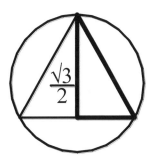

Figure 18a, The apothem in the equilateral triangle

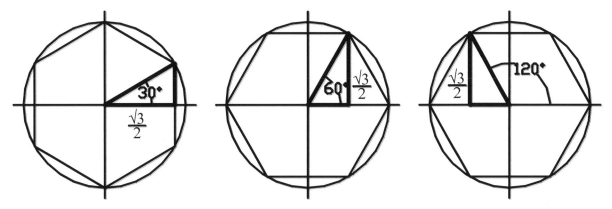

Figure 18b, Key lengths and corresponding angles in the hexagon.

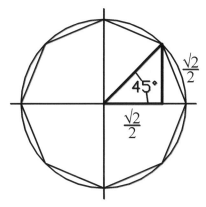

Figure 18c, Key lengths (equal) and corresponding angle in the octagon.

Finally, we look to the octagon, and graphically analyze it, as we also did with the hexagon (Figure 18c). We find in key trigonometric angles (also key angles used in astrology) the values of √2/2 and √3/2. These are related to 1/8 and 1/12, 1/6, and 1/3 of a circle, respectively (as shown by the geometries and use of the Pythagorean theorem). As our angle increases, rotating about the circle, lengths below the line would be considered negative, in graphing, but still have the same numeric values. The vertical lengths, divided by the radius (whose value here is consistently '1') form a proportion, which we recognize as Sine. Note that the vertical length is '0' when the angle is also zero, and is equivalent to the radius when the angle is 90°. These all provide various decimal answers when worked out on a calculator. But kept in fractional form the following revealing trigonometric table can be obtained:

| Angle | 0° | 30° | 45° | 60° | 90° | 120° | 135° | 150° | 180° | 210° | 225° | 240° | 270° | 300° | 315° | 330° | 360° |
|---|---|---|---|---|---|---|---|---|---|---|---|---|---|---|---|---|---|
| sine | $\frac{\sqrt{0}}{2}$ | $\frac{\sqrt{1}}{2}$ | $\frac{\sqrt{2}}{2}$ | $\frac{\sqrt{3}}{2}$ | $\frac{\sqrt{4}}{2}$ | $\frac{\sqrt{3}}{2}$ | $\frac{\sqrt{2}}{2}$ | $\frac{\sqrt{1}}{2}$ | $\frac{\sqrt{0}}{2}$ | $\frac{-\sqrt{1}}{2}$ | $\frac{-\sqrt{2}}{2}$ | $\frac{-\sqrt{3}}{2}$ | $\frac{-\sqrt{4}}{2}$ | $\frac{-\sqrt{3}}{2}$ | $\frac{-\sqrt{2}}{2}$ | $\frac{-\sqrt{1}}{2}$ | $\frac{\sqrt{0}}{2}$ |

Table 2, Sine values, in fractional form making a pattern of roots.

While it is easy to work with Pythagorean triangles, the associated angles are decimal, such as: 36.87°, 53.13°, 22.62°, and 67.38°; found in the first two triangles. There are in fact no cases (other than 0°, 90°, 180°, 270°, and 360° – which are not triangles) where a whole numbered angle will give a whole number ratio between sides in the triangle. But, the commonly used trigonometric (and astrologic) angles provide a square root–of–a–whole number relationship! Again, not random in nature, they focus on √2/2 and √3/2, with inclusion of √0/2 (which is '0'), √1/2 (which is '1/2'), and √4/2 ('1').

## The Sine wave

We can rotate around a circle by these varying angles, maintaining the radius and seeing these positional numbers such as √2/2 and √3/2 (above or below, to left or right, of the crossing axis). But, what if our frame of reference were moving, "coming out of the page" as it were, as we do this rotation? Imagine a tube, with a coil of wire wrapped around it. The "radius" of this spiral is still the same. Looking straight at it, it seems still to look like a circle. But, if we changed our viewpoint to be from the side, what would the image look like? A sinusoidal wave (Figure 19).

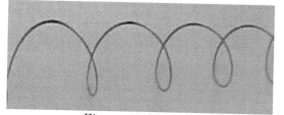
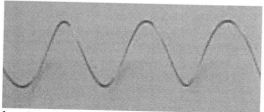

Figure 19, The spiral; two views, clearly showing the sinusoidal nature.

A lot of things adhere to the sinusoid, which we wouldn't normally consider. As shown in Figure 20, there has long been an understanding of this, relative to the movement of the nighttime sky.

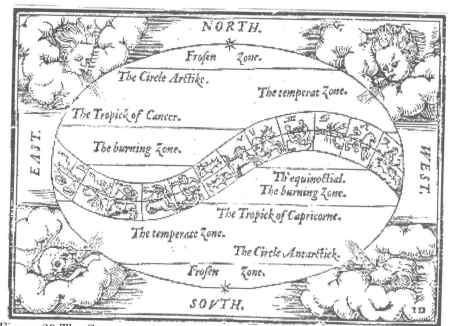

Figure 20 The Cosmographical Glasse (William Cuningham, London, 1559).

How does the Moon move about the Earth? A circle? We teach this in school and nothing could be further from the truth. The Earth is also in motion, which would require a massive acceleration and 14 days later deceleration of the Moon; generated by some external force, which just doesn't exist.

Actually, the motion of the Moon is elegantly linked to that of Earth. Both are accelerated centripetally such that they do not get sucked into the Sun's gravity. Their paths intertwine. When Moon's motion carries it beyond the Earth, the parent tugs back on it, slowing it down until the Earth catches up and passes by. Now will the Earth pull on it again, accelerating it; a process which begins at each new moon, followed by the brakes being gravitationally applied at the full moon.

Moon's motion could be more accurately described in Figure 21. Is it possible that the Natives of North America knew this a thousand or more years ago when they built Serpent Mound in Ohio? Moon's motion reflects these images with one more addition; that it would be simultaneously rising out of the page and sinking back in, again as though around a tube (rolled into a ring). Actually, there is one further addition: the Sun is also moving, rotating around a central point in the galaxy. It's all in motion – circular spirallic!

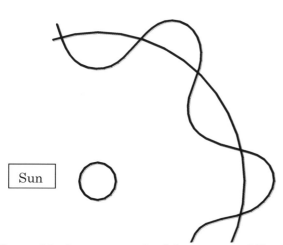

Figure 21a Apparent path of the moon and Earth.　　21b Serpent mound – (Squier and Davis).

As above, so below; the Macro and the Micro. Human DNA strands, in the double helix reflect the dance of Earth and Moon, and other planets with their satellites – particularly the "planetoid" Pluto with its Charon, nearest in size *and* distance of all parent – satellite combinations in our solar system. Spirals and helixes are also found in plasma strands of electromagnetic energy emitted and received by the Earth's magnetosphere; part of the complex ionization of our atmosphere, upon which the rains are dependent.

Figure 22, The double Helix (wiki). Birkeland currents (NASA)

We are taught that AC current flows in a sine wave. But, we need to realize that currents of sound, light, and electricity flow outward from a generating point, as we see when we drop a rock into a pool of water. The initial pulse pushes water away, whose movement creates a vacuum, drawing back on the water. Returning water molecules collide and repel, repeating the pulse effect; breathing in and out. If we could cut through this image and rotate it by 90° we would see the sine wave. But, in the medium of air and space, the pulsing occurs spherically, emanating from one point in an infinitude of three – dimensional directions. In the cylinder of a wire, the pulse or movement of an electron would follow the helix spiral, seen as a sinusoid from the side.

Why is it that metal cables and fiber ropes are stronger when the strands are wrapped spirallically? Tree trunks and branches can also exhibit this.

## From other Angles

We may notice from Table 2 what is missing from the angle pattern, though not from the Sine pattern. These are the angles such as 15°, 75°, etc. In our high school trigonometry we studied something called half-angle and sum formulas. These are usually not taught in any way that would make them appear interesting in the least. But, if we look at them in a creative context we find that they have values such as these: $(\sqrt{(2 - \sqrt{3})})/2$, and $(\sqrt{(2 + \sqrt{3})})/2$. Interestingly, half again of 15°; 7.5° gives Sine/Cosine values of $(\sqrt{(2 \pm \sqrt{(2+\sqrt{3})})})/2$. Looking at these mathematical terms too long can make many cringe (better to look at mandalas). But the point is that the formulas we saw in school were developed perhaps thousands of years ago and were meant to solve problems such as these, by people who were philosophizing about math. Mostly, we should be seeing that these angles are rigidly held to values incorporating $\sqrt{2}$ and $\sqrt{3}$. There is more in Chapter 6.

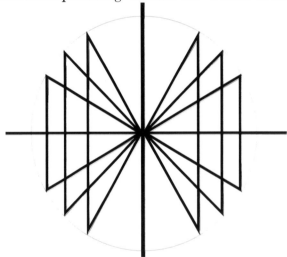

Figure 23, A "mandala" of the key trigonometric angles. Imagine the mind in the center!

The math we are taught in school is *not* fulfilling us. The student who rushes to solve answers and thinks that this means something is filling Ego, temporarily. The scientist who creates advances (*always* exploited then militarily or economically) is just an overgrown extension of this. Is it any wonder that the techno world being created by mathematicians and scientists, and being bought up by All, is bereft of humanity and regard for nature when we are not teaching mathematics philosophically; not seeing the Sacredness within?

Well, perhaps the mathematical exposure so far has not convinced the reader of an association between mandala, math, and the Sacred. It is *still* only introductory. Hopefully it has at least not been boring. Please enjoy the next chapter...

And now a few pieces of art to bring us back to wholeness:

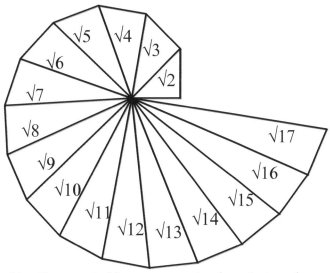

Figure 24a, Nautilus created by square root values (outer edges measure '1').

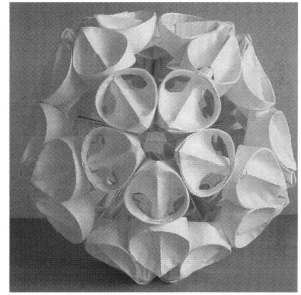

Figure 24b, Beauty in geometry: Octahedron Pattern created from 32 folded paper plates.
Icosahedron Circles (60 plates) Part of "Wholemovement" – courtesy Bradford Handford-Smith.

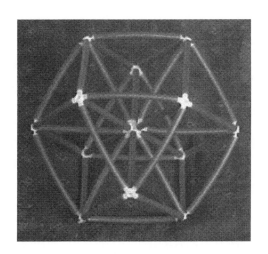
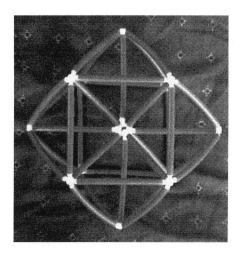

Figure 24c, Two views of the Cube octahedron (in the dark). Note Star of David, hex, and square.

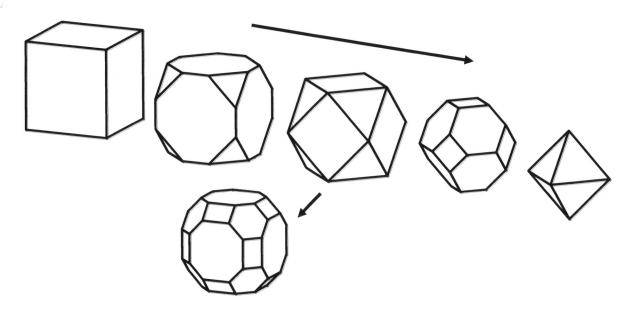

Figure 25a, Progression from the cube to the octahedron, thru various Archimedean forms

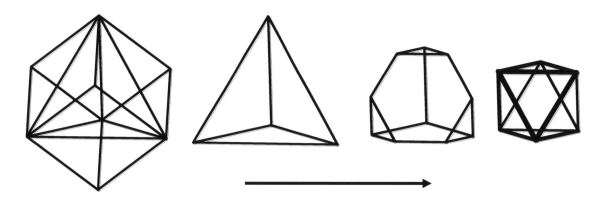

Figure 25b, Progression from the cube to the tetrahedron, truncated tetrahedron, and octahedron.

We have studied the geometries of the five Platonic forms but those of the thirteen Archemedic shapes are interesting in their greater depth of complexity, all of which can be reduced to mathematical expressions based on square roots of fairly simple numbers.

In Figures 25a and b, we see the development of various Archimedic forms, generated by trimming from the cube. One form mutating into the next. Many times, placement of the cuts are at logical points, such as one third the edge length, or $\sqrt{2}/2$ units from a vertex. Notice that trimming both a cube or a tetrahedron can result in an octahedron!

It is interesting to make these forms, from paper or perhaps zometools. Figure 25c shows the flat patterns for various fold-ups of Archimedean bodies. Notice their mandalic structure.

Calculation of the geometries of these forms can be rather complex. However, their radius-to-edge proportions work out to functions of $\sqrt{2}$, $\sqrt{3}$, and $\sqrt{5}$; with such values as $1 + \sqrt{5}$, $\sqrt{(2 + \sqrt{2})}$, and $x + y\sqrt{5}$. Again, scientific rather than random values (though more involved).

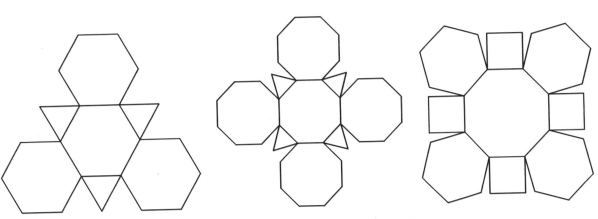

Figure 25c, Patterns for three Archimedic forms.

Finally, in Figure 25d, notice the play with two platonic forms. In the tetrahedron, it is interesting that each removed piece is in the shape of an octahedron.

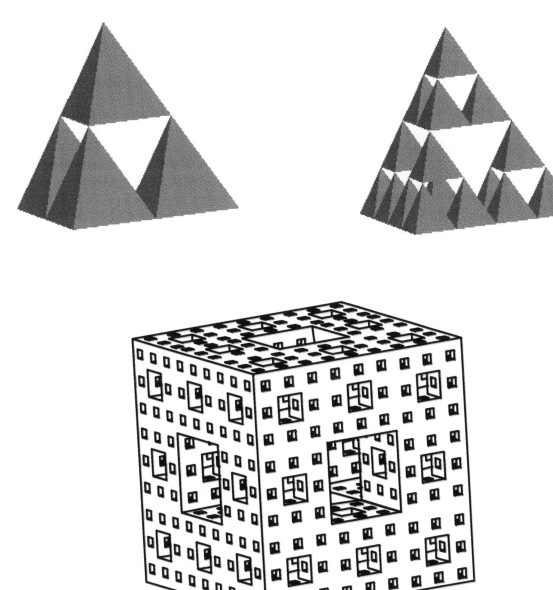

Figure 25d, Surgery performed on two basic 3D forms.

Figure 26, Further ideas, like a 16 – fold pattern, or Metatron's cube; named after a biblical angel.

Figure 27, Hand work.

Our minds are capable of amazing creativity, as shown in the preceding diagrams. Eventually, we should break free from the compass and ruler, or use them only a little, seeing what practice, and then free – hand can create.

# Fifth Chapter – 5

Sacred geometry is Sacred Proportion, or the comparison of two lengths. We can pick a number, and have a friend give us another, totally at random; for example 4 and 25. If we add them, the smaller to the larger; to get 29, and then the larger of that first pair to the first sum we get 54. We continue then, always adding the result of an addition to the larger of the pair which made it: 83, 137, 220, 357, 577, etc. We can divide any number in the resulting sequence by the previous number. At first the answers can vary, sometimes by quite a lot. But, as we develop our sequence, usually around the thirteenth number divided by the twelfth, we converge on a value of 1.618. Any two numbers, regenerated in this fashion will end up with the same result, which is fun to run in a group of people.

A renaissance man named Fibonnacci is credited with mostly discovering a specific sequence which not only does this same thing, but which appears to be a counting pattern of growth in many plant species, and reproduction rates in the animal. Fibonnacci is also the one to have brought Arabic (Indic) numbers and counting into Europe, so that mathematicians could add numbers like we do Today, instead of still using Roman numerals. The Fibonnacci sequence is: 0, 1, 1, 2, 3, 5, 8, 13, 21, 34, 55 etc. We use it each time we play on a piano. Here, each 1 octave consists of groupings of 2 and 3 (5 all together) black keys, interspersed with 8 white, making 13 in total.

We can use this sequence to build a spiral, growing ¼ arcs each by a radius according to values in the sequence. This is shown in Figure 1.

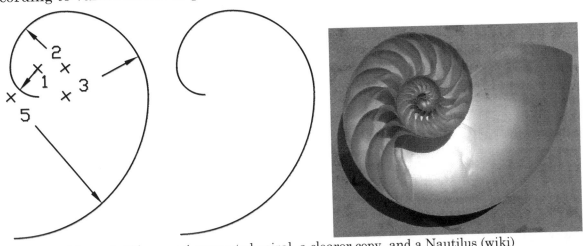

Figure 1, Fibonnacci generated spiral, a clearer copy, and a Nautilus (wiki)

All spirals can be created mathematically, just as any straight or curved line for that matter. Let's generate a list of all of the places in nature where we might find spirals: your thumb print, ear, crown of your hair, curls, the tracing of a circular line along the side of your nose, up and over your eye and then down along your chin, fern fronds, grape tendrils, sea horse and pig tails, nautilus/snail shells, tornadoes, water running down the drain, fetuses, pine cone (look at the patterns closely on one), flower petal whorls, sheep horns, high pressure/low pressure systems, and galaxies. Granted that not all of these are according to the Fibonnacci sequence but it is clear that spirals are a naturally occurring phenomena and can be created by our sequence. We can use it to make a few things (Figure 2a).

Yin and yang can consist of two dancing spirals; two complimentary energies. A symbol commonly found in cathedrals is the triskelle (a Greek word), often found in Celtic – Irish art, used to represent the Trinity. The third is the swastika (a

Sanskrit word originally), symbolically used in almost every culture from the dawn of time; to represent the Sun mostly but also peace. Its modern usurpation has led to its banishment in the West (but not East); unfortunate considering the deeper meanings originally associated.

Figure 2a, Common symbols using 2, 3, and 4 spirals.

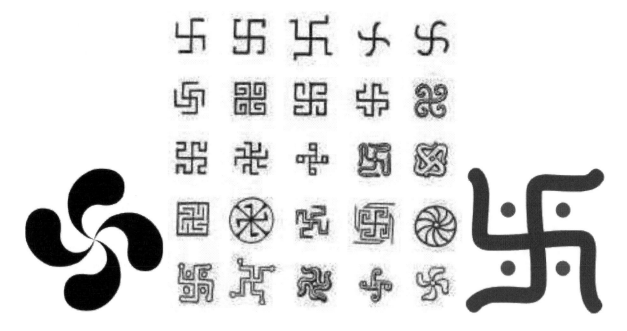

Figure 2b, A variety of historical svastikas from around the world (wiki).

## The Spiral

The spiral has long been held sacred by Humans. Modern researches believe that its presence at ancient solar temples is a form of writing; indicating Sun. In Figure 3a we see spirals found at New Grange, in Ireland; at the main portal, in the "womb" of the temple, and at the other axial end, aligned to the winter solstice sunrise 5 – 6000 years ago, to receive the reborn energy of the Sun. This temple's front is encased in quartz crystal.

Figure 3a, Spirals found on the axis of the Sun at New Grange.

Carved spirals upon a rock are found in the equally antique temples of Malta and further afield. Native Americans at Chaco canyon carved them on Fajada Butte, towering at the entrance to their ceremonial land. Not only did they etch several spirals on its peak, but they erected three great menhirs in such a way that sun and moon light could shine between and around them. Noon time sun specifically interacts with the spirals, as shown in Figure 3b; summer solstice, winter solstice, and equinoxes, respectively. Solar and lunar rises on key dates will cast an angular shadow that interacts with the spiral form uniquely at each time.

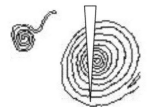
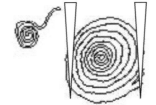
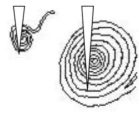

Figure 3b, The so-called sun dagger effect on the Spiral.

On a separate face of the butte, a further spiral also denotes light beams of the sun, interestingly piercing the double spiral before/after and during spring and autumn equinoxes.

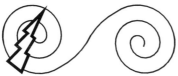

Figure 3c, Sun dagger effect before/after and at the equinoxes.

The spiral, serpent, and dragon are all connected archetypal themes of rebirth, sun and life. In historic and modern cultures dragons are thought to exist in the land, sky, and sea. If we believe that we have a soul which continues after we pass is it not possible that the angels, faeries and such mythological beings could also exist? The spiral, snake clans and serpent/dragon in myth around the world all indicate a subliminal – primordial connection we have to energy and how it flows.

The story of Patrick casting the serpents out of Ireland is metaphor for him pulling the people away from their pagan beliefs in dragons (druids were associated with them) and native energies. St. George slaying the dragon also echoes the "triumph" of a modern belief system over the former. Again metaphor, it may reflect how modern views the Natural, how we still today are crushing nature and those indigenous people still trying to maintain their sacred link to it. These people have tens of thousands of years of the Sacred tied into their DNA, most symbolized in the serpent and spirals found in their art, etched in their stones, and painted on their bodies. What else does the spiral represent for us?

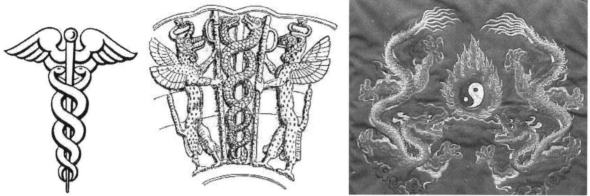

Figure 3d, Double Serpents and dragons; Caduceus, Sumerian Ningizzida (wiki), Chinese dragons.

The spiral abounds in Nature, seen and unseen, in the micro and the macro. The serpent is often used as its representation. The kundalini energy is thought of as a sleeping serpent, at the base of the spine, to be awakened, ready to link heaven and Earth.

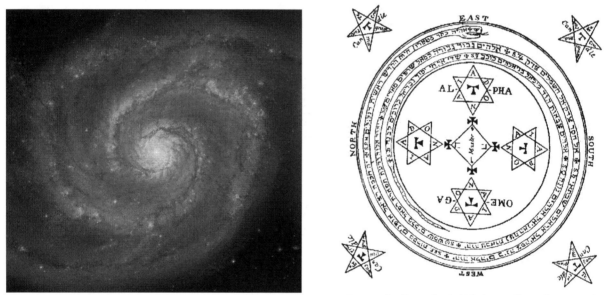

Figure 3e, Spiral galaxy M51 (NASA JPL). The Serpent in symbolic spiral (Aleister Crowley 1904).

## Proportion

Let's work further with the spiral, mirroring just one. We see then in Figure 4 the result. The heart shape can be found in nature: leaves, petals, and cut across varieties of fruit such as the apple, cherry, peach and plum.

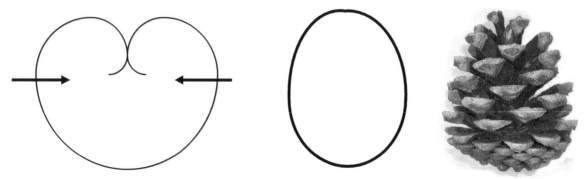

Figure 4, Two mirrored spirals. As the spirals come together - leaves, egg and pine cone (wiki)

As we have worked with two, three, and four spirals, let's now work with five, rotating them also around a central point but in a different fashion. Figure 5 shows the result of this: a flower echoing the blossoms of the rose family. This is almost

Nature's blueprint for edible foods, as the previously mentioned fruits, plus rosehip, pear, raspberry, blackberry, strawberry, and apricot all concur. Interestingly, if one looks under the blossom at the green portion of the bulb, which has split open, there lurks a 5-pointed star. Nature can guide us (The origin of this word comes from the ancient Egyptian word for spirits around us, the Neteru).

Figure 5, The five-petalled flower, and the star geometry it reveals.

We will proceed now to construct a 5-pointed star, going from the curves of the feminine to the linearity of the masculine. To do this, we need an aid, which is the vesica piscis we made earlier.

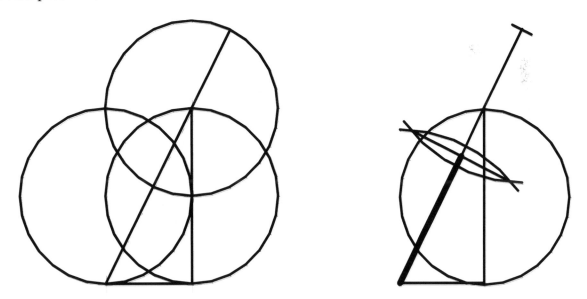

Figure 6a, Use of the vesica piscis to generate three important numeric values.

Using a radius of '1' in the circles, we should remember that the long diagonal measured '√5'. We already worked with the "lesser" radical values at length in the previous chapter. Now we'll use this one. In Figure 6a we will extend this line by another '1', using a circle centered at its extreme to do this (left image). In the right image, unneeded material is removed so that we can focus on this line, bisecting it to find its center. The length of half of this line can be derived by Pythagoras, and then division. It is (1 + √5)/2, which has a numeric value of 1.618. This is the exact number that our earlier sequences will converge on. It has been found to be very unique to mathematics, and nature, and for this reason has been assigned a Greek letter and name; Φ – phi (which some scholars call Tau – τ). Often times this has been called the golden mean, or golden section. Section because it is the place on a line where we can cut; such that the proportion of the longer piece to the shorter is exactly the same as that of the whole to the longer piece. The proportion of the two is 1.618 and the place on the line will be 0.618 units from one end. This latter is the result of dividing '1', by Φ (Figure 6b).

Figure 6b, The golden section.

We next use two of the dimensions given in Figure 6a, taking lengths of exactly '1' and Φ by setting our compass to them. Note, we can generate the vesica piscis of any size, merely calling our radius '1'. If we use one inch, or one centimeter, the drawings tend to be too small. A very good quantity to use, as will become apparent, is a radius of '2.25' inches.

So, again create a vesica piscis, radius '1' (actually '2.25'). Make a larger circle centered on the leftmost, of radius 'Φ' (left image Figure 7). Draw lines from that shared center out to the points of intercept given on the right circle. These are construction lines. Where they cross the left circle is a new unit of measure to which we set our compasses. If we are very *very* precise, we will end up being able to generate five equally spaced marks around the left circle.

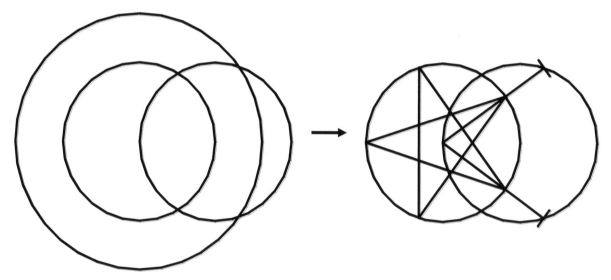

Figure 7, Generation of the 5 – pointed star.

These five marks enable us to draw a perfect star. Measuring the lengths of the pentagon contained within that star (if we used '2.25' as our unit '1') will show them to be exactly '1' (relative to the scale used for 2.25). Measuring out from any corner of the pentagon to the tip of the star will give 1.618; though this precision is not measurable given our rulers, though we can in fact come pretty close (Figure 8).

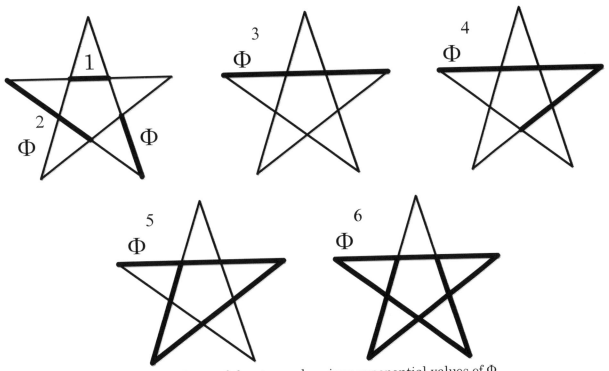

Figure 8, Parts of the star and various exponential values of Φ.

This is only the beginning of the fun we can have with the star. Again, the length across the pentagon is '1', and a star leg length is 'Φ'. Their sum is 2.618. If we take the square root of this on the calculator, we find that it returns us to 'Φ'. So, $1 + \Phi = \Phi^2$. This statement is a mathematical anomaly, which does not occur for any numeric value other than Φ, and its negative inverse: If we use the quadratic equation learned in high school (again *real* application), we obtain $(1 \pm \sqrt{5})/2$, giving numeric values of 1.618 and $-0.618$.

| Leg addition | Φ exponent |
|:---:|:---:|
| $0 + 1\Phi$ | $\Phi^1$ |
| $1 + 1\Phi$ | $\Phi^2$ |
| $1 + 2\Phi$ | $\Phi^3$ |
| $2 + 3\Phi$ | $\Phi^4$ |
| $3 + 5\Phi$ | $\Phi^5$ |
| $5 + 8\Phi$ | $\Phi^6$ |

Table 1, Phi values.

Further "play" with the star opens our knowledge of Φ. As we trace around a given star, we see that a sequence of counting develops to arrive at each exponential value of phi. For example, the fourth exponent consists of two pieces of the pentagon, and three legs of star tips. Hence, we obtain '2 + 3Φ'. If we tabulate the results of counting thusly, we see an interesting pattern develop, as shown in Table 1.

The table shows us, interestingly, that the exponential values of phi reveal the Fibonacci sequence; two of them! Thus, the sequence converges on the golden mean, whose exponents return to the sequence. Again unique to this number.

Play with the numerical value of phi; $(1 + \sqrt{5})/2$ also reveals something interesting. The reader is spared the math but many of those rules we learned in high school have again *real* application here. Their use results in Table 2.

| Radical value | Equivalent | Radical value | Equivalent |
|---|---|---|---|
| $\dfrac{1 + 1\sqrt{5}}{2}$ | $\Phi$ | $\dfrac{-(1 - 1\sqrt{5})}{2}$ | $\dfrac{1}{\Phi}$ |
| $\dfrac{3 + 1\sqrt{5}}{2}$ | $\Phi^2$ | $\dfrac{3 - 1\sqrt{5}}{2}$ | $\dfrac{1}{\Phi^2}$ |
| $\dfrac{4 + 2\sqrt{5}}{2}$ | $\Phi^3$ | $\dfrac{-(4 - 2\sqrt{5})}{2}$ | $\dfrac{1}{\Phi^3}$ |
| $\dfrac{7 + 3\sqrt{5}}{2}$ | $\Phi^4$ | $\dfrac{7 - 3\sqrt{5}}{2}$ | $\dfrac{1}{\Phi^4}$ |
| $\dfrac{11 + 5\sqrt{5}}{2}$ | $\Phi^5$ | $\dfrac{-(11 - 5\sqrt{5})}{2}$ | $\dfrac{1}{\Phi^5}$ |

Table 2, Radical values of phi exponents and their inverses.

Looking to the columns, we see again the Fibonacci sequence, but also a new progression of numbers which behaves similarly: 1, 3, 4, 7, 11,... If we finally look to Table 3, we see something interesting about this new sequence.

| Number | $\Phi$ relation |
|---|---|
| 1 | $\Phi^1 - 1/\Phi^1$ |
| 3 | $\Phi^2 + 1/\Phi^2$ |
| 4 | $\Phi^3 - 1/\Phi^3$ |
| 7 | $\Phi^4 + 1/\Phi^4$ |
| 11 | $\Phi^5 - 1/\Phi^5$ |

Table 3, Examination of the new sequence.

Sacred Geometry includes mathematics. There is no way around it. One of the amazing "coincidences" in math is this particular proportion. Unfortunately, our educational process is silent here. Its inclusion has been shown to be very exciting for youth.

Trace the 5-pointed star to explore its magnificence. Where do we find this star in nature (Figure 9)? In Human use? Symbols of high military rank, national flags, white magic, black magic, natural magic, US military, level of quality, Chinese 5-element theory.

 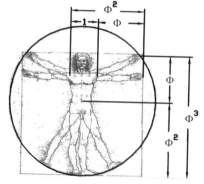 

Figure 9a, Phi and five - related objects

The 5 – pointed star has long been used as a symbol by occultists, particularly in the Tarot as the suit of pentacles. It is finding renewed use today by Wiccans, but has long been used to represent "white" magic. Satanists have inverted it and used it as well, unfortunately offering outside observers a chance to misconstrue one for the other.

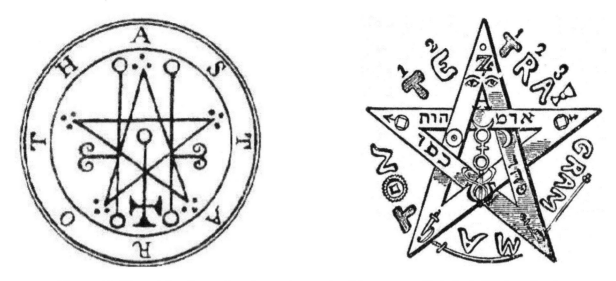

Figure 9b, Use of the five pointed star in magic, (Macgregor, Crowley), Eliphas Levi

Much more has been outlined in We as Architects, and other books and so is not repeated here. To summarize in lieu of repetition; the proportion is roughly found in multiple divisions of the body; for example the relative lengths of the individual bones in a given finger, back to the wrist, a person's overall height relative to their "belly-button" height, head height to width, and also arm length versus shoulder width. The proportion is found approximated in the relative spacings of the planets around our Sun, and of the regular moons which orbit around Jupiter and Saturn.

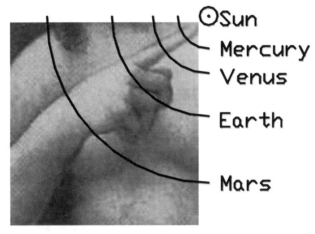

Figure 10, Spacing of the planets from the sun.

Imagine a cloud of dust particles in a very large portion of space. Particles and bodies, free to float are manifestly attracted to each other. This is mundanely referred to as gravity. The particles do tend to move in a direction to others, bonding chemically and ionically. The motion is not linear but *spirallic*. As more and more material gathers, some center forms, into which much of the material is further drawn. More and more (much more) comes in, over a very long time, even in a cosmic perspective. When enough mass is attained, the whirling mass ignites into one gigantic fusion reaction; a star.

Eddies within the currents of this star-building spin off, also gathering material. This congeals into spherical shapes, spaced outward from the star. These objects orbit with the direction of spin of the star, but they may or may not spin on their axis in this same direction. In our case, Venus spins opposite and Uranus is tilted at just over 90° to the plane (line a ball rolling instead of a top spinning).

Each "birthed" planet might have moons of its own, which also spun as eddies around the parent body. In both cases, the spherical bodies are spaced out according to the same proportional spacing of the joints in our hands.

## Acknowledgement

Many ancient mystery schools are thought to have stressed that Universal Laws are expressed within the Human constitution. With phi we find this may be true, meaning the faces of friend and stranger alike reflect a map of the universe.

The key thing to understand about phi is that when we look for it in Nature, we often as not find it (at least approximately); in the proportions in the body segments of a bee, or the growth of leaves on a stalk; a spiral. Growth itself is so very often spirallic, eg. the kernels in a pine cone or sunflower.

We are surrounded by chaos, but within the maelstrom lies order. Pull back the veil to reveal more chaos, and then again order, as though the layers of an onion. Phi is one mathematical definition of that order.

The Sacredness which is Geometry is the Sacredness of the spheres that have formed: one as Sun, who nourishes us and the other life forms − of the physical, devic, and angelic realms; one as Earth, who feeds and clothes us; one as Moon, who somehow balances our psyche and regulates our rhythms; and the host of planets whose "music" plays a symphony to our soul and who act as archetypes and guides. We see the sphere in the dandelion, ready to spread its seeds upon the ground. This "lowliest" of weeds is also one of the most healing.

The mandalas, stars, and other geometric drawings and forms which we create are our Mind's attempt at joining and participating with the Sacred Mind within all of the Creation around us.

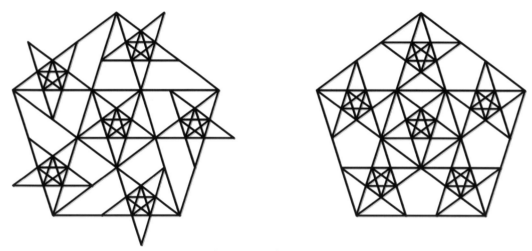

Figure 11a, Fractal images of stars, showing their ease.

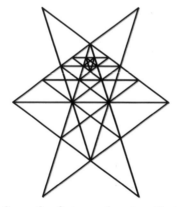

Figure 11b, Growth of stars, showing their interaction.

88

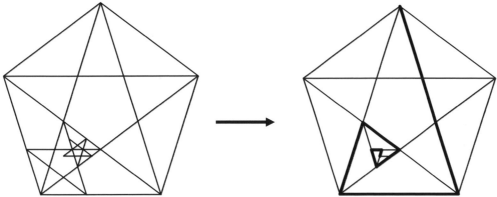

Figure 12a, Creating a phi spiral in the star.

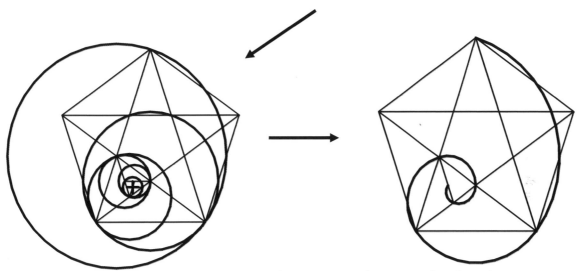

Figure 12b, Curving the spiral in the star (Note the center of each circle).

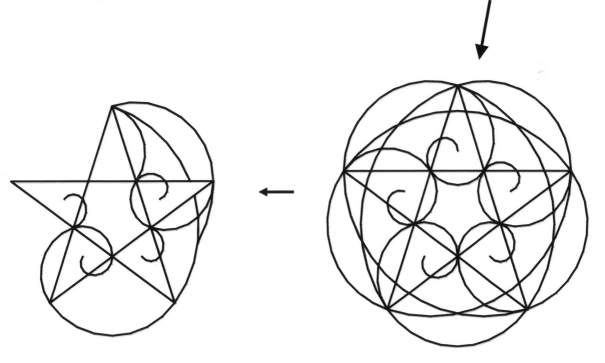

Figure 12c, Something different (left image) and multiple spirals (right).

Figure 12d, Draw multiple spirals, mirror, and then erase.

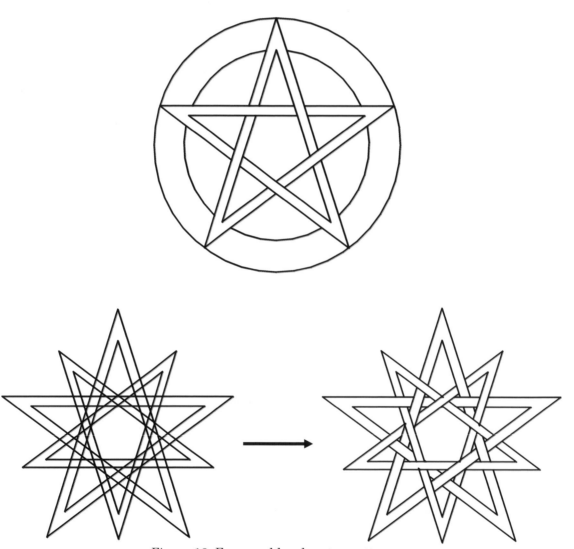

Figure 13, Easy, and harder star patterns.

**Mind in 3D**

We have left one of the Platonic forms until now, due to its relative complexity in construction, and also its relation to phi. Thus, we will now proceed. In the interest of simplicity, we should now make a circle whose radius is 4 and 1/4 inches. This requires either finding the exact center of the page, and/or accepting that portions of the circle will run off the paper. This is actually not a problem because the entire circle is not needed. This length is the best at making the next step with a regular value. Make a top mark and then change the compass size to 5 inches (if using metric set the compass to 8.5 and 10 cm respectively). Proceed then around the circle to get all five points (99.9% accurate).

With the five points, draw the 5 – pointed star which incorporates them, and also the pentagon which encompasses it (Figure 14a left image). Following the progression shown, we draw lines across the central pentagon, extending outward to the larger (central image). Finally, erase the star from the middle and cut out the pentagonal form shown in the right image.

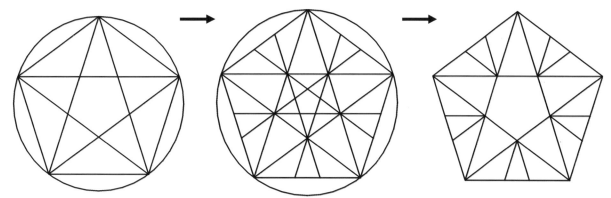

Figure 14a, Drawing steps and cutout.

We now have two routes through which to proceed. These are demonstrated sequentially in Figures 14b through f. In the left column of diagrams, we should make two pieces, which will mate. For the right column; twelve pieces that will attach. Note, a harder stock of paper should be used for this and the designs should ultimately be colored while flat. Glue a string inside...

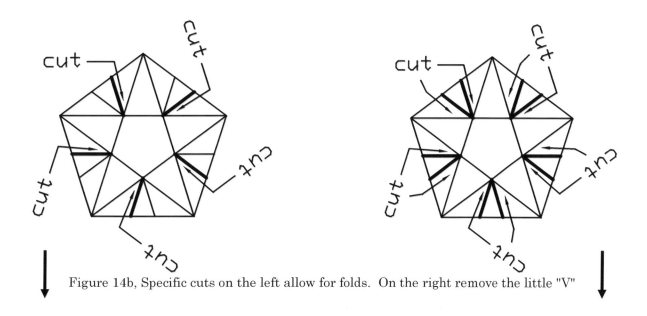

Figure 14b, Specific cuts on the left allow for folds. On the right remove the little "V"

91

fold
bold
lines

fold
bold
lines

Figure 14c, Fold each pentagon and winglet on the left. On the right fold all the wings around each triangular leg and then fold the leg itself inward.

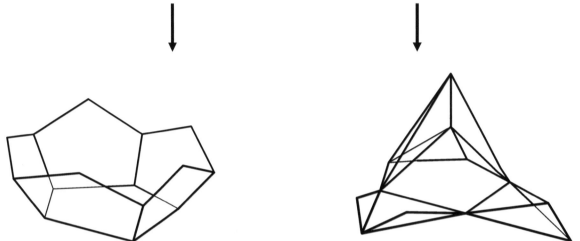

Figure 14d, Fold and make a cup on the left. On the right; "pyramids" (thinner lines are hidden)

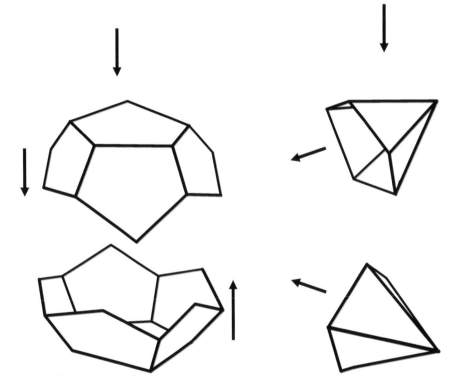

Figure 14e, Two cups make a dodecahedron. Attaching the twelve pyramids is optional.

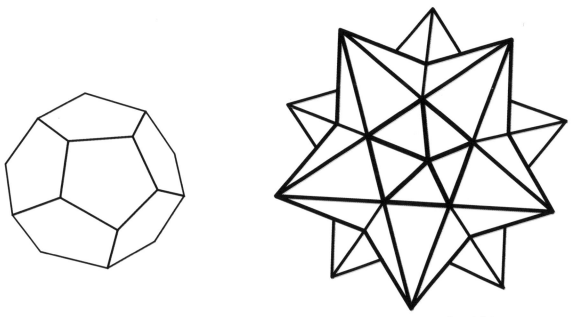

Figure 14f, The dodecahedron on the left.  Its stellation on the right.

When the stellation is complete, notice that there are essentially twelve 5 − pointed stars, each along some unique axis.  There are 60 legs in this stellation, each leg a factor of 'Φ' longer than the edge of the dodecahedron which it extends.  Count the points.  There are twelve, the same as the number of vertices in the Icosahedron.  Note that between groupings of three star tips could be placed an equilateral triangle.  These star points define an icosahedron!

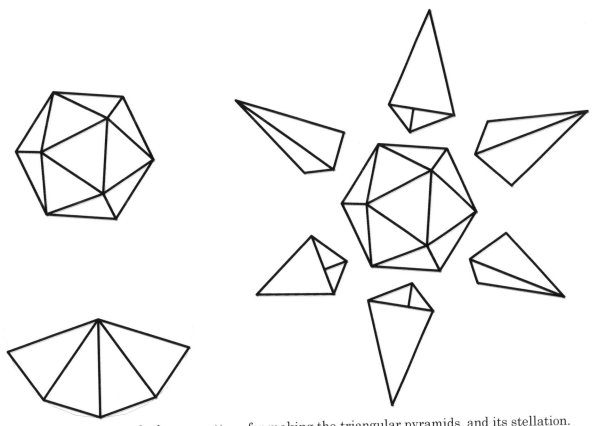

Figure 15, The icosahedron, a pattern for making the triangular pyramids, and its stellation.

We can also stellate an icosahedron, as demonstrated in Figure 15.  Here, draw a partial circle whose radius is a factor of 'Φ' larger than the edge of the icosahedron which it will extend. Make marks around the circle with a compass set to the edge length of said icosahedron. Cut out, fold, and glue it on! Here there will also be 5-pointed stars, along 20 axis (also 60 edges). The points define pentagons; the faces of a dodecahedron which could be created from them. Hence we have shown that the two are duals of each other. Also, the 5 – pointed stars confirm the presence of phi in both. Remember the onion: stellate one form to get the next, which is then stellated to return to the former, two harmonics larger.

In Figure 16 we see how phi is demonstrated within these forms. If one were to cut out three rectangles whose proportions were 1:$\Phi$ and intersect them through each other in three axis, all points of an icosahedron are defined. If we do the same process with rectangles of 1:$\Phi^2$, there will be defined three of five points of each pentagonal face of a dodecahedron.

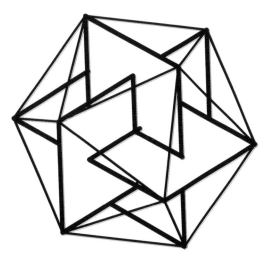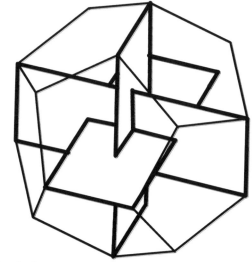

Figure 16, "Phi rectangles", and the Platonic forms they define.

The fact that there are three axis perpendicular to each other, ending in linear edges having a parallel opposite partner indicates that an octahedron could be constructed connecting the midpoints of each of these edges (which would lie on the faces of a cube). The dodecahedron can incorporate all of the Platonics, including a tetrahedron! With 20 points, we may insert five separate tetrahedrons, spiraled around each other, as demonstrated with zometools in Figure 17.

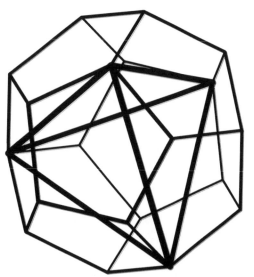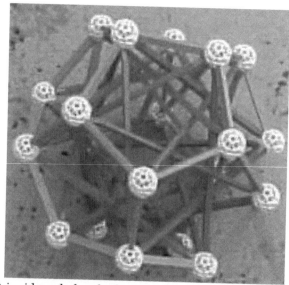

Figure 17, The tetrahedron(s) inside a dodecahedron.

The fact that octahedrons and tetrahedrons fit inside these forms can only mean one thing: Φ, √2, and √3 must be related. They are, as demonstrated in Table 4, where we again are given the final conclusion, without all of the math. Still, doing the math, for the mind that is interested and capable, is a fascinating process of discovery, which astounds the mathematician with patterns. The reader may wonder where a person finds the time for such pursuits. Indeed! Notice the similarity between √2 and √3 values and the radii of the icosa – and dodecahedron. In the next chapter we will see an interesting parallel.

| Number | Φ relation | Number | Φ relation |
|---|---|---|---|
| Roots: | | Radii to edge: | |
| $\sqrt{2}$ | $\sqrt{(\Phi^3 + 1)}/\Phi$ | icosahedron | $\sqrt{(\Phi^2 + 1)}/2$ |
| $\sqrt{3}$ | $\sqrt{(\Phi^4 + 1)}/\Phi$ | dodecahedron | $\sqrt{(\Phi^4 + 1)}/2$ |
| $\sqrt{5}$ | $\sqrt{(\Phi^5 + 2)}/\Phi$ | | |
| $\sqrt{6}$ | $\sqrt{(\Phi^6 - \sqrt{5})}/\Phi$ | Other | |
| $\sqrt{7}$ | $\sqrt{(\Phi^8 + 1)}/\Phi^2$ | $\sqrt{5}$ | $\Phi + 1/\Phi$ |
| | | $\sqrt{5}$ | $\Phi^2 - 1/\Phi^2$ |

Table 4, Phi patterns.

The five pointed star, and the proportion which rules it, can provide no end of explorational opportunity. Figure 18 provides one final example.

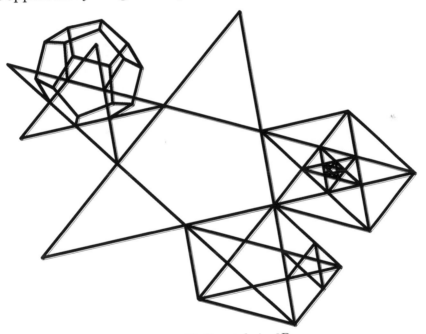

Figure 18, Fractals in 3D.

These forms really need to be experimented with. A product like geomag is good because the balls and magnetic struts show how strong the tetrahedron is, and the octa – and icosahedrons (must be the triangles). Yet the cube is pretty "wobbly", indicating that the boxes we spend our time in are actually comparatively weak. Further, the dodecahedron simply collapses under its own weight.

Secondly, something like zometools should be used, starting with an icosahedron whose edges are the shortest blues. This will allow for construction of its stellation; the dodecahedron which is then defined, and its stellation, so that the layers can be seen in all their glory.

Figure 19, Duals from Tubespace; stellated octahedron in the cube, icosa – in the dodecahedron.

Finally, a new product called Tubespace is good in that the nodes have legs which contain double the amount needed. These are very handy for building the duals.

## Seven

In five – fold geometry we have demonstrated exhaustively concrete ties to Phi. Let's return now to the geometries created in Figure 5. We will go through a similar process as in Figure 7, but this time using radii of 'Φ' and '2' (Figure 20).

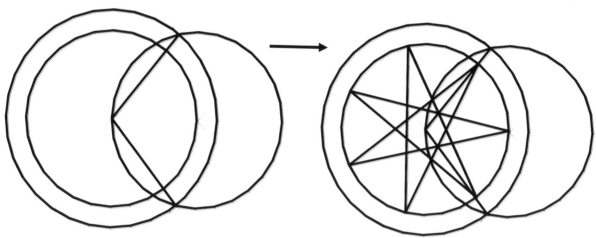

Figure 20, Creation of a seven point star.

With a lot of precision we can use phi to make a 7 – pointed star also! Almost. The result is better than 99% accurate, and that is the thing about 7, and phi, there are a lot of "almosts". As we work now with seven, we may wonder if these almosts are close enough. After all, the spacing of the planets and the proportions found in the body are also almost, and even less accurate.

Seven was a number held by the ancients in high esteem. Alchemy and astronomy for a very long time were structurally held around seven. As we have seen earlier, 7 is a mystic number. We notice it by its absence (along with 11) from the list of numbers, 1 to 12, with which we may readily work. These two values; 7

96

and 11, are the relative heights and widths of the great pyramid (actually 280 Egyptian cubits by 440). Using them; as 22/7, one finds the Egyptian value for pi, 99.96%. Also, 14/11 is very near to $\sqrt{\Phi}$; 99.94%. Thus, both classic proportions seem built into the great pyramid; as best as one may do. The angle then created is 51.85°, which is 99.2% of one seventh of a circle – the closest division one may obtain with any whole number.

This one seventh of a circle opens up a myriad of tantalizing curiosities. Stonehenge is located essentially at this latitude, to observe solar maximum sunrises, which occur there at the *same* angle, to North. Due to astro mechanics, this is phenomenally at 90° to the lunar maxima here. This is the only latitude on the planet (north and south) where this occurs. This angular difference is 60° at the great pyramid. Key angles. A similar special agreement between angular alignment and latitude occurs at one other latitude; which is half of 51.5°, or one fourteenth of a circle. Here, the Egyptians built Karnak, a contemporary of Stonehenge. Later, American Indians built the immense Newark circle at a latitude which would incorporate similar angles relative to the moon, indicating that varied cultures from around the world, in varying times held some fascination with seven – fold division; some sacredness.

Particular among them were the Mithraists, who kept seven stages of initiation. In more modern times, seven – fold mathematics has been important to the Masonic movement, in the placement of Washington DC and other state capitols at nearly 38.5° North; the complementary angle to 1/7th of a circle (besides no part of the US can be found at 51.5°). An interesting astronomical fact is that 60° separates sunrise maxima at this latitude. These are facts associated with Earth, and its tilt, tying in seven with all of the unique numerology and geometry we have been reviewing; which are universal. Almost as though seven is the micro, while 3, 4, 5, 6, 8, 12, and 16 are the macro.

Regarding the masons, their commonly used symbol of an eye in a pyramid is found throughout Baroque Europe, mostly as the symbol for God, in cathedrals. This pyramid is made in the same proportions as the great pyramid in Egypt. A similar form is found on the US $1 bill, but this time drawn more specifically to seven – fold geometries. See Figure 21 where we see the fall of Man, should he/she listen to the serpent and seek wisdom...

Fun can be had dividing by 7, looking for patterns. The first thing we find is a repeating pattern of 142857. The second is that each fraction "jumps" into this sequence at some point, before continuing with the repetition (Table 5). So, while seven is not heavily tied in with all of the numerical oddities we've been reviewing, it has some of its own.

| 1/7 | 0.14285714285714... |
|-----|---------------------|
| 2/7 | 0.285714285714... |
| 3/7 | 0.42857142857... |
| 4/7 | 0.57142857... |
| 5/7 | 0.7142857... |
| 6/7 | 0.857142... |

Table 5, Division of 7.

We will include seven in our work, because it does bring in further geometries, any of which have their own beauty, as shown in Figure 22, where we mix two inverted 7 – pointed stars with two 5 – pointed counterparts. Seven is also part of our psyche.

Figure 21, Adam and Eve and the garden of Eden, with the all-seeing eye, accompanied by 7 – pointed stars.  Stone carving, Worms cathedral.

Figure 22, Five and seven fold interplay.

To draw a 7 – pointed star from scratch, a delightfully close approximation can be obtained with √3 (again, one of those "almosts"). Draw a square of any desired leg length, calling this "unit 1". The diagonal will have a length √2 times longer. Draw on this a rectangle whose perpendicular leg measures again '1'. The new diagonal, by the Pythagorean Theorem will measure √3. Bisect this to get √3/2. Set the compass to a radius of this "unit 1", make a circle, choose a top mark, and with the compass set to '√3/2' find that it is possible to make 7 marks around the circle (99.7%).

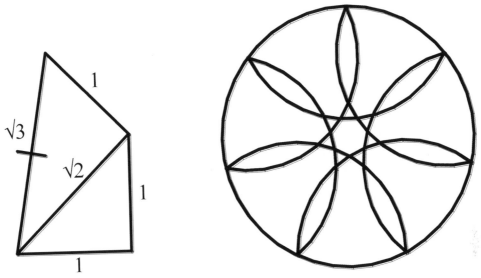

Figure 23a, Find √3; bisect it. Then do a circle of radius '1'. Finish with marks spaced at '√3/2'.

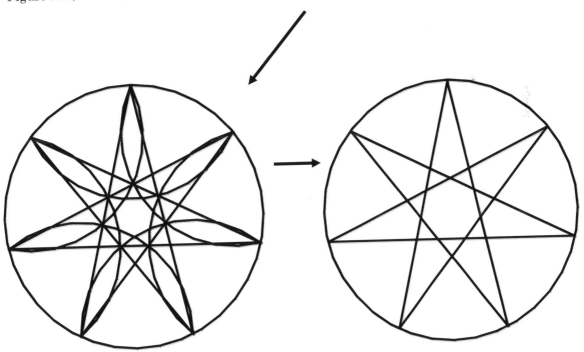

Figure 23b, Play with the form, ultimately finishing with a 7 – pointed star.

Stars of 5, 7, or more points add to the shapes we can create in our Sacred Geometry experimentation. Certainly it has been demonstrated that five – fold geometry has tremendous mystical potentialities. Does seven? If we study the Vitruvian man, by da Vinci, we do see something interesting in this unique artwork, as shown in Figure 24a.

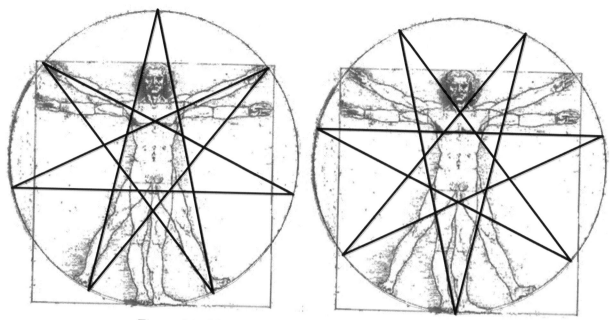

Figure 24a, The Vitruvian Man, with a 7 − pointed star.

Print out a copy of this drawing. Make a top mark on the circle and try to get a seven pointed star. Interestingly, it is possible to see faint marks on most pictures that are already there. Marks of the master. Did he use this geometry to create the form, or is it inherent to Human anatomy? Both? Let's continue, using 8 − fold geometry (Figure 24b), and even 9 − fold (two stars, side by side, side oriented).

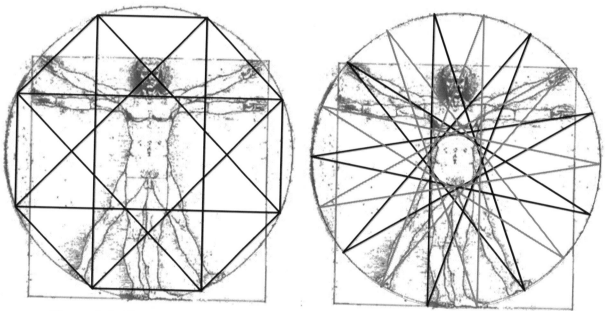

Figure 24b, The Vitruvian Man, with a 8 − pointed star, and two 9 − pointed stars.

What these various stars do is show key placement and proportion of the body, in this drawing, which is said to be one of the most proportionally correct pieces of art ever created. Is the geometry that we see demonstrated here the reason?

If we perform a similar study of Stonehenge, very interesting geometries are revealed here as well; when using the enigmatic 56 hole pattern thought to have been used to calculate eclipses of sun by the moon. This architectural work would have predated da Vinci by 30 centuries.

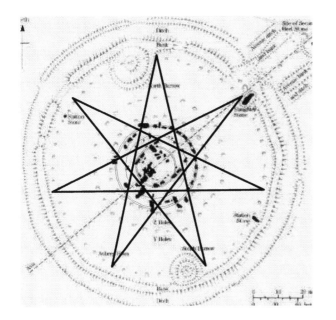
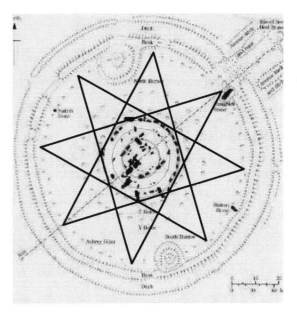
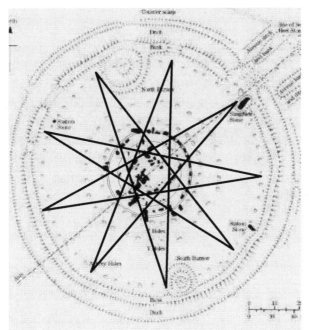

Figures 25, A study of geometries at Stonehenge.

What is most interesting about these geometrical overlays is that the 7 and 8 pointed stars appear to define the outer ring of standing stones, one touching upon their inner radius, the other on their outer! And then the 9 – pointed star appears to describe placement of the stones in the horseshoe.

How did the ancients lay out circles of such size? Were these geometries so important to them that they left them hidden in plain site for us?

What did they know, that we have fallen asleep from? We will see one more thing, in the next chapter.

Imagine Stonehenge when it was newly built, its massive blue-gray stones looking over the plain. The sky starts to lighten; a faint blue, and birds are singing. Facing to the North east there is a glowing brightness, while to one's rear the sky is duller, darker. The horizon starts to lighten more, its edge gleaming. And then the green glow gathers up and explodes as a point of golden light stabs at the far horizon. Slowly the sun begins to rise, and about the time that its entire disk is above the horizon the observer must close their eyes to the sight.

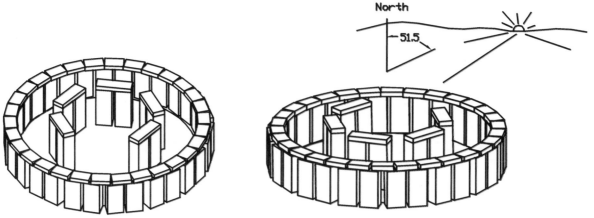

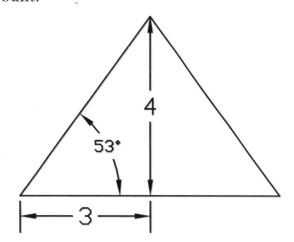

Figure 26, Stonehenge; two views.  Note 51.5°

The Sun rises each day in a different spot, readily noticeable in spring time after only a few days.  In Summer and winter, leading up to and then after each solstice, the sun rises for nearly three weeks at the same place; its maxima.  The Moon too has such maxima, yet two things are different about it.  First, they are further to North, or South, by a few degrees, and second, they are harder to predict, occurring at approximately 19 year intervals and irregular times.

Research makes it appear that all major cultures; be they Mesoamerican, Egyptian, Sumerian, or Megalithic, built their temples (pyramids or circles) aligned with some solar or lunar maximum.  This is a reasonable endeavor but moreso is the astro-mechanics associated in the geometries and *latitude* selection.

The 3 x 4 x 5 triangle is a fundamental geometric construction.  The musical fourth has the ratio of 3:4.  We find this is the form of the internal construction of the second largest pyramid at Giza, companion to and almost identical in size to the Great Pyramid.  This is also the latitude on our planet where New Grange was built.

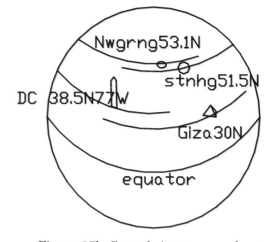

Figure 27a, The second pyramid at Giza.                 Figure 27b, Sacred sites on our planet.

The Giza plain, in Egypt, sits at near-precisely 30° North.  Is it possible that the builders of Giza and New Grange were talented enough to know their latitude?  That in itself would be remarkable.  Moderns should wonder more, how did "mud – hut" civilizations have so advanced mathematics?  What was their science and, simply, why?  Further, the slope of the great pyramid is essentially the same as the latitude and angle of solar maxima of Stonehenge.  Figures 27 show key mathematical features of these sites, and their location on our Earth.  Notice the relation that 51.5° (and its complement; 38.5°) has to $\Phi$ and $\pi$.

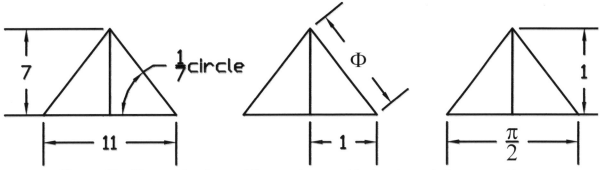

Figure 27c, Three side views of the great pyramid, showing relative proportions.

See how 60° separates solar and lunar maxima at Giza. This angle is 90° at Stonehenge. An angle of 60° (30° north and 30° south) separates summer and winter solar maxima at 38.5° North, where the Masonic fathers of the US placed their capitol (at 2 x 38.5° West) and many ancient sites may also be found (such as the Azores, the hypothetical remnant of Atlantis). Isn't it something that Earth's tilt accommodates 4-, 6- and 7- fold geometries?

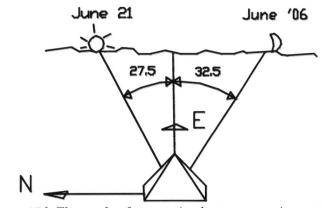

Figure 27d, The angle of separation between maxima at Giza.

The angles of 30, 45, 60 and 90 degrees are easy and key to mathematics. Yet why did the ancient mysteries determine that sacred sites be situated such that they correspond to 51.5°? The giant circles built by the Native Americans in southwest Ohio were similarly aligned, but to a lunar maxima of this "phi" angle. Interestingly, their circles were built on a massive size, in which (coincidentally) the four corners of the great pyramid of Egypt would contact. The large pyramid of the sun in Mexico is very nearly also this size (off by a few percentage points, and the ratio of its height to base is essentially half that of the great pyramid in Egypt; hence, also phi (and pi) proportional.

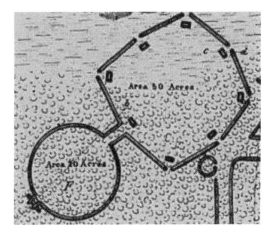

Figure 27e, The Octagon at Newark, Ohio, (Squire and Davis).

Imagine the winter sunrise at the temple of Karnak, in Egypt. The first rays of the Sun shine through the west-south-western gate. They strike upon a platform, contained within a stone home, whose walls are carved with reliefs of the priests welcoming the Lord Ra to come and sit at this table. The rays in that instant reach further, for this one room structure is open along both ends of this axis. The rays pass along a channel at this temple complex, flowing between the beautiful red-granite obelixes, full of hieroglyphics, through one pair of massive pylons, the columns of the court, another pylon pair, another, along the avenue lined with sphinxes, across the Nile and off to a temple at the Valley of the Kings.

All of this is set up to 25.75° of angular alignment (from East) and Latitude. This angle is half of our 51.5. This temple, contemporary to Stonehenge (where Egyptian artifacts have been found), shares the fact that at no other latitude does that latitude agree with the angular relation of Sunrise maximum, with respect to either the East or North.

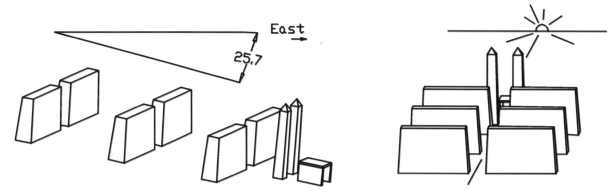

Figure 27f, The temple of Karnak.

As each major culture had its temples, each aligned to some quality of Solar and Lunar aspects is it possible such places were all part of a global astro-study carried out thousands of years in the past? It is known that these sites are built on ley lines, but modern researchers suggest that they are on key Earth nodes, intersections of a grid of major energy lines flowing round the Earth, according to a regular geometric form of course. Sacred geometry, art, architecture, *and* geography.

## Artwork

We can do our usual creative work with seven; as in Figure 28a. Here, seven 7 – pointed stars have been drawn around a central point at their vertexes. See how the stars interact with each of their neighbors. Some erasure enhances the drawing. A similar process can be performed with 5 – pointed stars, where the stars seem to be "arm–in–arm", though not as intricately (Figure 28b). Though five presents us with phi, seven presents more complexity. Beside the 5 – pointed are shown nine 9 – pointed stars rotated about a center formed by their vertices. Not only an explosion, but again interaction and greater complexity, which is not unattractive. Note that some lines in these drawings become shared.

So, it appears that while five has provided us such a wonderful demonstration of the Sacred found in Geometry, there lies greater complexity and perhaps discovery in the higher harmonics of seven and nine.

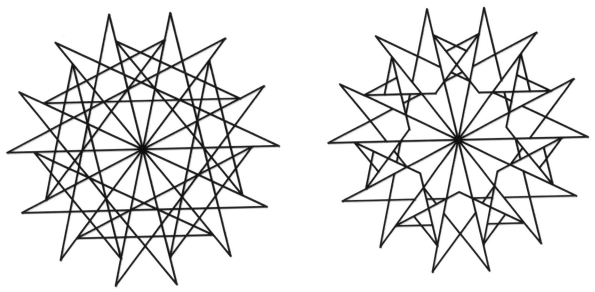

Figure 28a, Seven – fold rotation.

Figure 28b, Five – and nine – fold rotation (nine is enlarged to show detail).

## The Sri Yantra

Yantras are an interesting Indian geometric device. With all of our other drawing efforts, we should include this. Return to Figure 5 for specific dimensions. Lightly draw a line across the center of a page, exactly "2 units" long. From either end, swing an arc of measure 'Φ'. Top and bottom intercepts denote the apex of two large triangles, proportional to the Great Pyramid (Figure 29a). We then draw a circle whose center is upon the middle of that original line, extending or drawing further lines as shown.

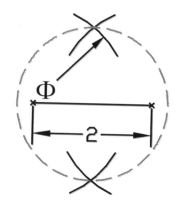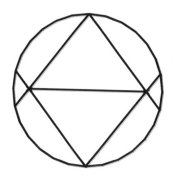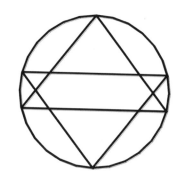

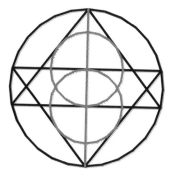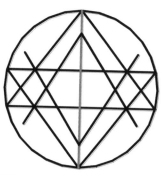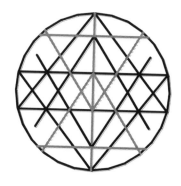

Figure 29a, Initial steps

We then draw a light line down through the center of the image. Two light circles can then be drawn internally to get key points. Notice then how these geometries are utilized (Figure 29b). Trim as shown.

Figure 29b, Crossing lines.

Ultimately, we can then finish the image, and put in further artwork around its border (Figure 29c). All of this thanks to phi!

Figure 29c, Finishing the Sri Yantra.

## Biology, geometry, and spirals

The field of physics has taken us far in understanding that energy movement in the world, and body, can be regular, vibratory, wave-like, and spirallic. The creation of spirallic and/or wavy lines might be particularly healing for certain organs of the body, mind, or spirit. The movement involved in making them creates harmonic resonance, exchanging energy and information. One modern body of work which uses this kind of energy movements is Dr. Ibrahim Karim's Egyptian system of BioGeometry(R); Dr. Karim has identified hundreds of these energy movement patterns, which he has trademarked with the name of "BioSignatures(TM)". It is interesting that such artwork has been part of the occult for some time. Further is where we find the spiral in the Human.

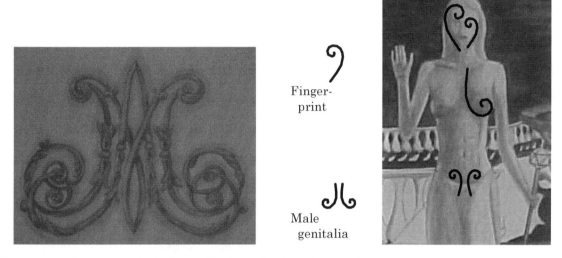

Finger-print

Male genitalia

Figure 30a, Spirals in the holiest of holies of a church, and the body (also ears, hair, and a fetus).

Figure 30b, Spirals we can draw. How could they be significant? What pathways might they open?

Imagine the healing of our body and soul through use of spirallic currents, and drawings. Imagine the sephirot as spirallic balls. So too the chakras. Just what level of complexity, unseen by our eyes, might these have?

Figure 31, Mandala, geo-art, chakra, figure 8? Could the "petals" of the chakric flowers be loops of energy, like electromagnetic bands wrapped around a planet? (One image, rotated in 3D space)

107

Cultures have long understood spirals, whether intuitively or with modern knowledge. The phi spiral relates mathematically to regular geometric forms, particularly the dodecahedron; easily stellated into an icosahedron, whose stellation returns us. Form based on specific harmonics. Growth, both physical and developmental, is often spirallic, as is energy flow. Key to us, vital energy is thought to have a spectrum, just like the visible colors of light, which repeats itself in ever higher octaves in various forms like the Platonic and Archimedic.

The spiral, the vortex, move energy to/from the periphery from/to the center. Geometric forms, particularly the sphere, contain energy and consciousness of various vibrations. The torus can be seen as a dynamic, though contained, field of energy. All of these forms can expand and contract, breathing in and out, retaining their shape.

Throughout this book are examples of 3D objects, which when viewed from a given perspective can appear as flat 2D forms or projections. Yet these are stationary. Picture sticks, standing at an angle above the plane. From above, they could look like a mandala. Yet, movement would create a "spirallic field" (see chapter 7 for an example).

Imagine our hands as a map of the cosmos. Our fingerprint contains a spiral. Our finger contains a message.

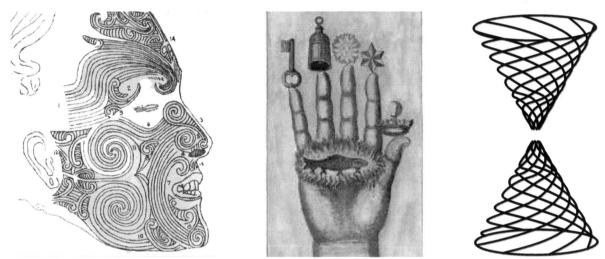

Figure 32, Maori spiral art, (John Rutherford, 1850), Hand der philosophen (J.l. Holland, 1773), and another possible form of the chakra.

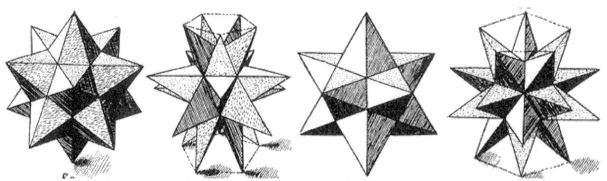

Figure 33, Further views of the stellated icosa – and dodecahedrons. (Kepler Harmonice Mundi)

Resonance is similar patterns, movement, or shape exchanging energy, in the harmonics of vital energy and dimensional levels. We need to further our understanding of energy, as Tesla and Reich have attempted to do. It was their belief that we are surrounded by usable energy, just put up an antenna or make a specially constructed box on the ground to collect it.

# Sixth Chapter – 9

Sacred Geometry is still awaiting discovery; or perhaps "rediscovery". As we saw in We as Architects, there is work we can perform as "creative", mathematicians and literary sleuths which might indicate not only the existence of an Atlantis, but of an actual high global civilization pre-existent to our own; perhaps possessive of higher technologies, including an understanding and experimentation with crystals in which we could be comparatively in infancy.

We see possibly some remnant of this in the crystallized stones found in many of the megalithic structures of the British Isles; which are among the oldest Sacred Geometrical sites erected on our World. There are many scholars Today who seem to think that our predecessors of 3000 BC in some ways possessed greater knowledge than millennia which followed, as though Humanity has digressed from some greater Golden Age (discussed in many mythologies) which preceded it.

We have seen in five – fold geometry the amazing laws which govern phi. We were introduced in seven – fold to the concept of "almost", and that while no particular mathematical proportion was presented, there is nonetheless a mystery and a regularity which can be found. That this appears to have been included in the building and location of Stonehenge, and other places, is reason enough to say "re – discovery".

Alright, maybe Atlantis did not exist, and knowledge the ancients held was not passed to them from some expiring predecessor. Then the question becomes, did these ancients possess a science, or an intuitive sense which steered them to these higher geometries?

Could they "perceive" atomic makeup, sound and light geometries, spirallic motion which we need technology to measure, "see", and understand? What was/is it about seven, nine, and other numerics that they built accordingly in their sacred sites, their calendar, alchemy, and religious symbolism?

One of the further, final (for now) fun things about seven is the form that can be made with seven sticks of equal length. Do try this at home (Figure 1).

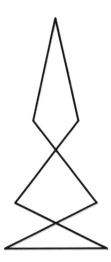

Figure 1, Seven equal length sticks and the form they can create.

We could have laid the seven sticks out in a "circle", making a heptagon. But this form is more involved. If we continue our play with it, we develop the forms shown in Figure 2.

Figure 2, Just some fun and ultimately beautiful work using 2, 7, and 14 of our "candlesticks".

When we overlay the "candlestick" on a 7 – pointed star, there is interesting concurrence. Too, if we would further install a vesica piscis at the base, there are an incredible number of points where the three forms interact.

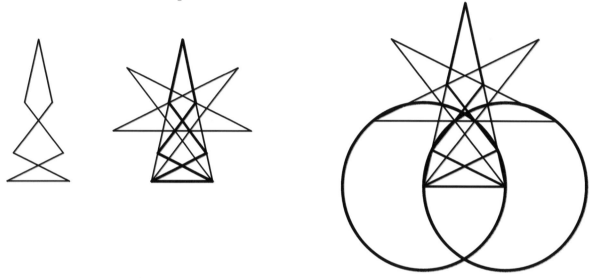

Figure 3, Sacred "science" found in seven.

Seven does not divide regularly into 360, to give us a nice angular reading. But, the pattern we saw presented by seven – fold division with its repetitive nature shows some "science" to be present. This science is further demonstrated in Figure 3, particularly that the vesica piscis rigidly defines eight points of seven – fold construction.

Seven is a number from shadow, hopefully brought somewhat into the light by this book. Seven is the number of days in the week, and of almosts. It takes 27.3 days for the Moon to find itself positioned again relative to Earth. Mechanically, it is not until 29.5 days that it "appears" to be in the same configuration. Seven is the number which most accurately divides into both of these terms, and so is not a bad designator for time keeping on our World. Four quarters to the moon cycle, each of about seven days.

**Lead in**

We can do a very similar process with nine, interestingly enough. And nine *does* divide regularly into 360, though a drawing means of dividing a circle by it *exactly* remains elusive. Progressing through the images in Figure 4, we see that our vesica piscis, with a third circle of equal size placed at their upper intersect, denotes also a great quantity of interactions.

110

Figure 4, Seven sticks, 9 – point overlay, and interaction of the vesica piscis.

Note in Figure 4 at the bottom of the "candlestick" that three segments form a triangle. This means that it is equilateral and hence all angles are equally 60°. This is seen as well by the interaction with the vesica piscis, how the lines converge at its top. Interestingly, the angle at the top of the candlestick is one third, or 20°. We have demonstrated in this book how to bisect, or divide by two, lines and angles, and also divide lines by three. But, modern mathematicians have yet to find a way to divide an angle into thirds. Figure 4 does not show how either. It simply does it!

We are going to dig into this further, scientifically, mathematically (a little), and artistically. The first thing we need to do is take a further look at the vesica piscis and geometric form.

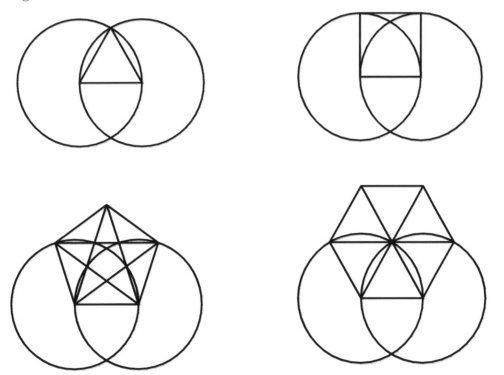

Figure 5, Triangle, square, pentagon, and hex; and interaction with the vesica piscis.

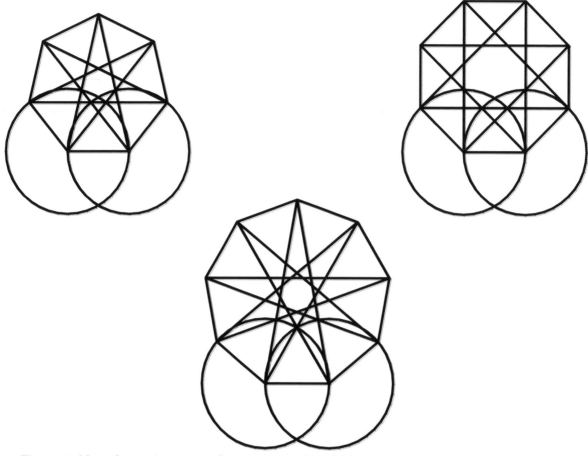

Figure 6, Note the various ways that 7–, 8–, and 9– fold stars interact with the vesica piscis.

In Figures 5 and 6, we see the generation of 3–, 4–, and 6– fold geometries easily determined by the vesica piscis, with work we have previously done. What is interesting in the higher "harmonics" is how the criss–crossing legs of the stars meet at points upon their respective vesica piscis. See in Figure 7, left, how 10–fold results in two 5– pointed stars, also interacting with the vesica piscis. In the right image we see 5– fold laid over 10– fold. Notice how the lines of the smaller pentagon, if continued would meet at vertexes in the decagon.

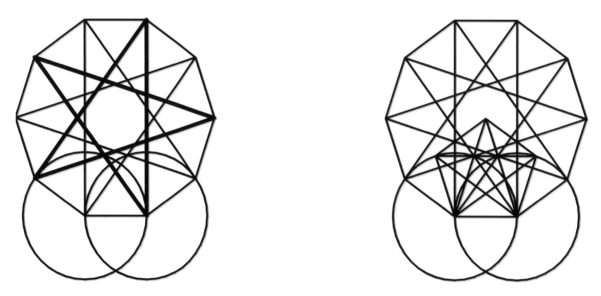

Figure 7, Ten– fold is two 5– pointed stars. Ten– and five– fold interact.

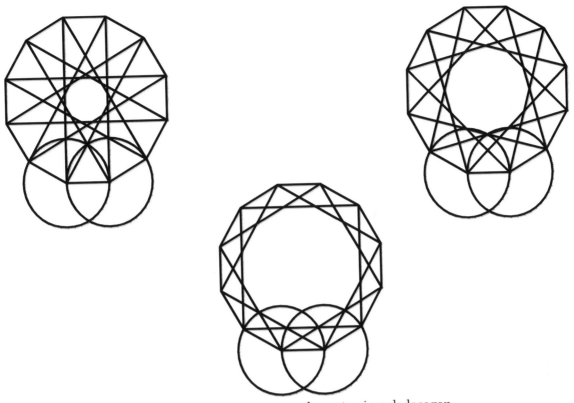

Figure 8a, Three ways to make a star in a dodecagon.

In Figure 8a, are shown the results of connecting points in the dodecagon in various manners; each of which has intersects upon the vesica piscis.

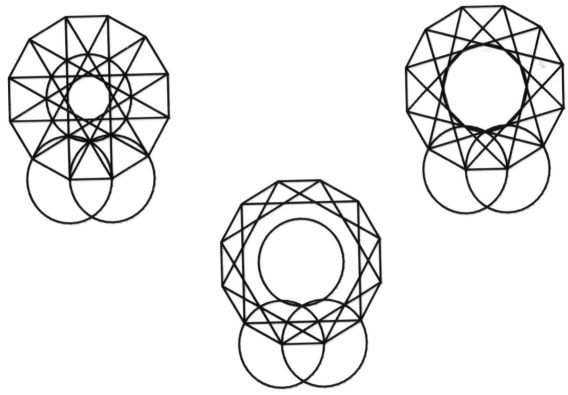

Figure 8b, The third circle.

We began working with the vesica piscis in the unit on phi. Now we see that it is indeed a dynamic construct, by how it can be overlain on top of all of these geometries. In Figure 8b, we will draw one more circle, whose radius equals the

113

circles in the vesica piscis, and which meets at their upper crossing point. It can be seen that the circle directly intersects the top two stars, centered within them! Finally, we see in Figure 8c, that it can indeed interact with the third.

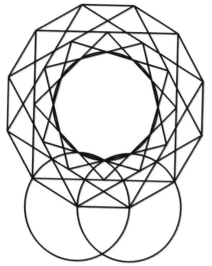

Figure 8c, Fractal meets the circle.

Figure 9, Six– and nine– fold overlaid.

This is all part of the "beauty" of Sacred Geometry; all of these coincidental crossings and intersections. What we are really after in this chapter is to be able to construct a 9– pointed star. Enroute, we will look at some mathematical facts, all part of removing the layers of the supposed chaos. First, let's notice that the hexagon can interact with nine– fold, as shown in Figure 9. We know the numbers in the hexagon well by this point; 1/2, $\sqrt{3}/2$, and 1. That it interacts somehow with this star would make us wonder if its geometry doesn't also work out to such "easy" numbers (note the "almost" point at the top center of the hex).

We should look at forms a little more in depth first, because mathematically, there isn't one that is bereft of some interesting feature. Take for example the 8– pointed star shown in Figure 10. With the inner square measuring '2' on a side, other key dimensions in the star (such as radial lengths to certain vertices) are revealed as being $\sqrt{2}$, or something having to do with a strange term of $\sqrt{2 + \sqrt{2}}$. Actually, this is not so strange (radius of the circle is $\sqrt{2}\sqrt{2 + \sqrt{2}}$).

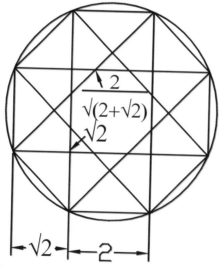

Figure 10, Key length relationships in the 8 – pointed star.

Those half angle theorems we learned in high school had a purpose, long since lost to modern teachers. In the preceding aeons without calculators, mathematicians knew easily how to get certain trigonometric ratios, as we have shown, for 30°, 45°, 60° and 90°. With the half–angle formula, their choices widened somewhat to such angles as 15°, 22.5°, and others beyond these 1/24th or 1/16th of a circle.

The cosine function, which is a proportion of the lower side to the hypotenuse, in the diagrams in Figure 11, works out to ($\sqrt{2 + \sqrt{2}}$)/2 for the angle 22.5°. Thus, the mysterious values from the center to the octagon are "simply" related. Note that in each point of the star the angles would be 45°; whose bisector is 22.5°.

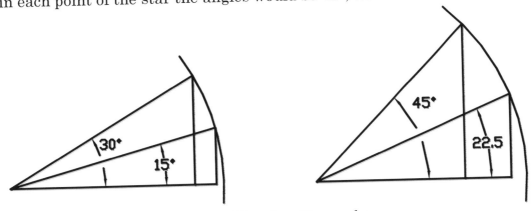

Figure 11, Bisection of key angles.

Working with the bisector of the dodecagonal angle of 30°, we find that the cosine of 15° will have a half–angle value of ($\sqrt{2 + \sqrt{3}}$)/2. Not only is this a similar value to the one seen above; but it is reflected in the following diagrams of a 12–pointed star (Figure 12a – b).

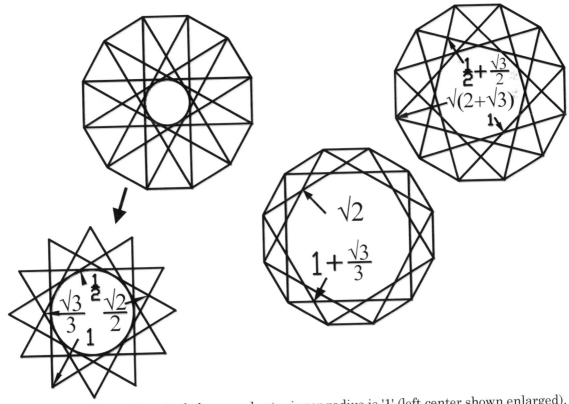

Figure 12a, Key dimensions in dodecagonal art – inner radius is '1' (left center shown enlarged).

In Figure 12a, we see a variety of radii with repetition of $\sqrt{2}$, $\sqrt{3}$, or some combination of them. If we look at various external lengths of the stars, we should be happy to see the result is very involved. But, underlying all is $\sqrt{2 + \sqrt{3}}$. See Figure 12b

115

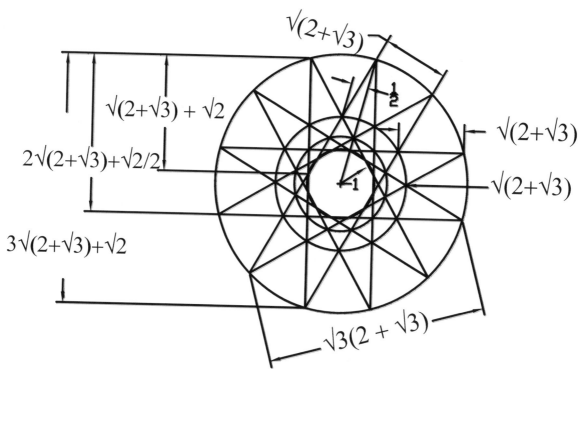

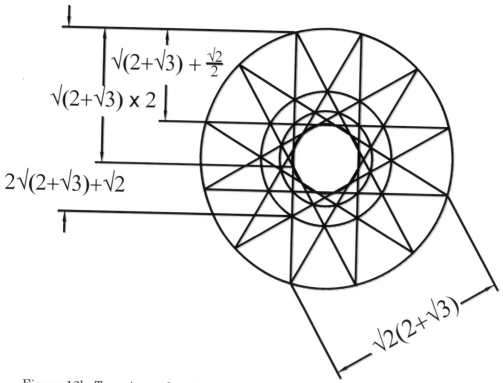

Figure 12b, Two views of various lengths, and their fundamental harmonic; √(2 + √3)

The most important thing for us to realize is that these various values might appear to be random (certainly, with a calculator, the decimal values do), but they are actually all functions of √(2 + √3); a complex proportion. Key is that these half angles (15° and 22.5°) relate to √2 and √3. Further half angles follow this, like the cosine of 7.5° being √(2 + √(2 +√3))/2. We see that again, part of the Sacredness of the Geometry lies in mathematics; with numbers we don't normally use.

**Nine**

In the 9 – pointed star each point is clocked exactly 40° around a circle. These two numbers are part of our factors of 360, but have been excluded from our study to this point. The reason being that this division doesn't work in with all of the other patterns we have seen so far; all but pentagonal division being strictly utilitarian as far as geometry and trig are concerned. We saw a lot of "mathemagic" with √2 and √3 (further uncovered just now for the reader), but the pure mathematician doesn't spend too much time on that these days, nor on all of that "phi stuff" in the 5– pointed star.

But, for all that modern math and science digs into, one thing they've never solved is trisection of an angle, like 60° to get 20°, or 120° to get 40°. And that is just the thing we need to do for 9– fold division. The author still hasn't figured it out either, but this is a problem that's been around for a while.

The thing that *has* been found is profound mathematics within 9 – fold geometry. Just as has been demonstrated in the chapter on phi, and the above work on different geometries, there is also a proportion at work in the nonagon. Its amazing parallel to phi in many arenas has earned it the moniker psi – Ψ.

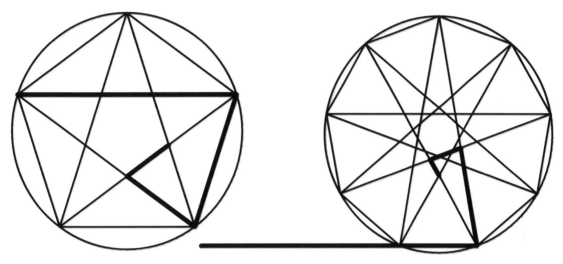

Figure 13a, Phi and Psi spirals, generated in their respective geometries.

Psi "behaves" a lot like its better-known cousin. We see this in Figure 13a, how it spirals around the star geometry, and in 13b where each leg of that spiral is seen to be larger by a factor of psi.

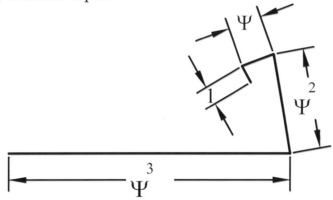

Figure 13b, Psi proportions found in its spiral.

So what is the numeric value? Reminiscent of phi; whose exact value is not only based on √5 but is also equal to 2 times Cos 36°, the value of psi can be found as the inverse of 2 times Cos 80°: 2.8794 approximately.

There are a number of ways that we can connect the points in the nonagon, as shown in Figure 14. With the "radius" of the nonagon set equal to psi we find that the various intercepts all are either functions of this proportion, or are '1' and '1/2'.

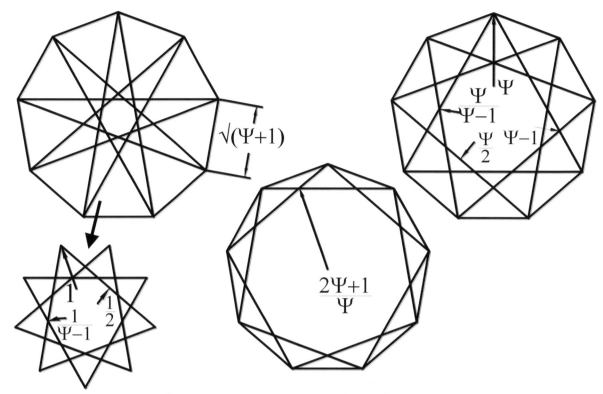

Figure 14, Psi in 9– fold geometries. The center of the left image is shown enlarged.

We saw that several numeric patterns occur around phi, particularly that returned us to either of two number sequences. Too, we found patterns relating to $\sqrt{2}$ and $\sqrt{3}$. With psi we find: $\sqrt{3} = \sqrt{(\Phi^4 +1)}/\Phi = \sqrt{(\Psi^3 +1)}/\Psi$. Similar in thought.

We obtained a value of $(1 \pm \sqrt{5})/2$ for phi from the equation $x^2 - x - 1 = 0$ (solutions were $\Phi$ and $-1/\Phi$). A similar equation: $x^2 - 3x + 1 = 0$ results in $\Phi^2$ and $1/\Phi^2$ and finally, phi can be found in this cubic equation; $x^3 - 2x^2 + 1 = 0$ (solutions here are the very "tidy" $\Phi$, '1', and $-1/\Phi$). A slight change; $x^3 - 3x^2 + 1 = 0$ will result in three answers also: $\Psi$, $(\Psi - 1)/\Psi$ and $-1/(\Psi - 1)$. Though these quantities are a bit more involved, they do result in $\Psi$ (or functions thereof) and can be found resembling the trigonometric values for 9– fold angles, as shown in Table 1.

|  | 2 x Trig value | Function of $\Psi$ |
|---|---|---|
| 2Cos 10° | 1.9696 | $\sqrt{(\Psi + 1)}$ |
| 2Cos 20° | 1.8794 | $\Psi - 1$ |
| 2Cos 40° | 1.5321 | $\sqrt{((2\Psi + 1)/\Psi)}$ |
| 2Cos 50° | 1.2586 | $\sqrt{((2\Psi - 1)/\Psi)}$ |
| 2Cos 70° | 0.6840 | $\sqrt{(\Psi + 1)}/\Psi$ |
| 2Cos 80° | 0.3473 | $1/\Psi$ |

Table 1, Cosine functions of nonagon angles (times 2).

Compare in the table the values for cosine of 40 and 50°. See too how these various cosine values are "sprinkled" throughout the 9– fold geometries, as shown above and in Figures 15a and b.

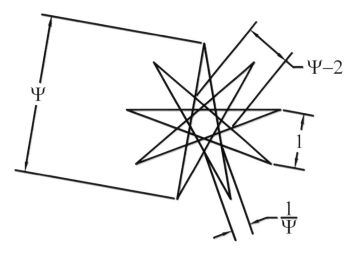

Figure 15a, Long side of the star measuring psi, and key related lengths.

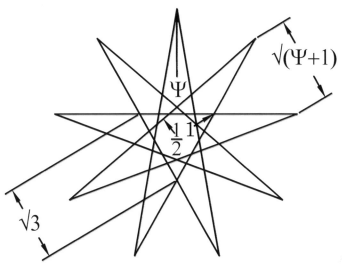

Figure 15b, "Radius" of the star measuring psi, and key related lengths.

It is tantalizing to see that '√3' and '1' are incorporated in the construction of this geometry. But, a "direct" square root solution remains elusive. "Almosts", as we will see when we go to construct the star. We are left with comparisons between triangular, pentagonal, and nonagonal constructions and proportions, as demonstrated in Table 2.

| Cos 30° (3 sides) | Cos 36° (5 sides) | Cos 40° (9 sides)? |
|:---:|:---:|:---:|
| $\dfrac{\sqrt{3}}{2}$ | $\dfrac{1+\sqrt{5}}{4}$ | $\dfrac{x+\sqrt{9}+\sqrt{(y+\sqrt{z})}}{8}$  ? |
| | | |
| Cos 21.2° (17 sides) | | |
| $\dfrac{-1+\sqrt{17}+\sqrt{(34-2\sqrt{17})}+2\sqrt{(17+3\sqrt{17}\ -\sqrt{(34-2\sqrt{17})}-2\sqrt{(34+2\sqrt{17})})}}{16}$ | | |

Table 2, Known and suspected values found in regular stars.

Notice the denominator of the known geometries; one less than the number in the stars. Notice too the root value correspondence to those numbers, and increasing complexity in the numerators.

Today, mathematicians insist that there is no other solution existing between 5 and 17. And yet, 3, 5, 9, 17 and 2, 4, 8, 16 are very functional patterns, suggesting that there should be. What is interesting is that Gauss discovered, *somehow* (and without a calculator), a solvable value for 17– fold division. This is

119

included here because it corroborates that something should work for 9, and that something is indeed missing from the pattern.

Finally, if we take the cosines of 1/18th, 2/18ths and 4/18ths of a circle (20, 40, and 80°) and multiply these disparate terms, we obtain a very "easy" '1/8' as the result. This may not seem like much except that it is the exact same result from multiplying cosines of 1/14th, 2/14ths and 3/14ths of a circle, thus suggesting a connection between 9– and 7– fold division... Were the builders of Stonehenge, Native American sites, and the pyramids mathematically advanced enough to realize any of this? Was da Vinci? Does this mean that all stars, particularly odd – numbered ones have a unique geometry, and proportion? Imagine, not one "phi", but an infinite quantity. And what about trisection?

As was said, no technique has yet been found for how to trisect an angle. In the star geometries however, we see that it simply does occur. And not just trisection! We will revisit our "candlesticks" (Figures 16).

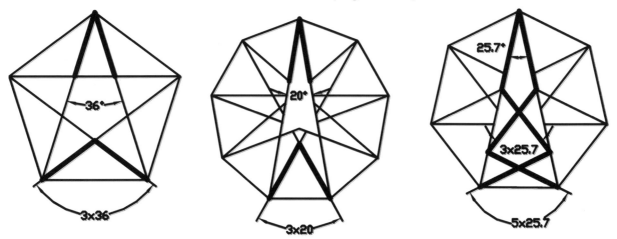

Figure 16a, Division of an angle by 3, and also 5! Demonstrated in stars.

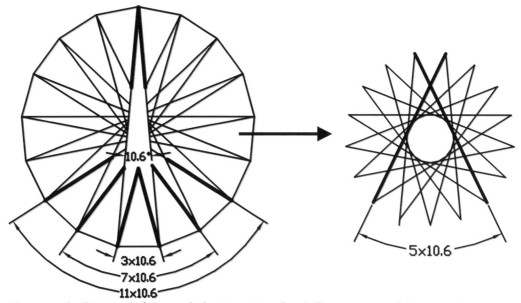

Figure 16b, Division of an angle by 3, 5, 7, and 11! Demonstrated in 17– point stars.

In Figure 16b the central portion of the star is shown enlarged, where all bold lines in this "candlestick" have the same lengths. More possibilities in 17!

We have on this odyssey through seven and nine found a phi-type proportion, discovered trisection of angles, and even further division; which math and science have as yet not found method for.

## Nonagon

Let us at least try to draw a 9– pointed star, and with it 18. We begin with a circle and a hexagon inside. Draw another circle to the right, which touches upon this at one point. Draw lines across the hexagon, continuing across the second circle (Figure 17a). Draw two sets of further lines; the first pair of which should go from the center of the first circle to those distant intercepts on the second. This angle will be very nearly 20° (99%). The second pair of lines should radiate out from the center of the first circle, through the hexagon; touching tangentially on the second circle. Finally, draw a large circle, centered at the first, which meets the distant intercepts. This will define two, or four, points in a nonagon, or 18 – gon.

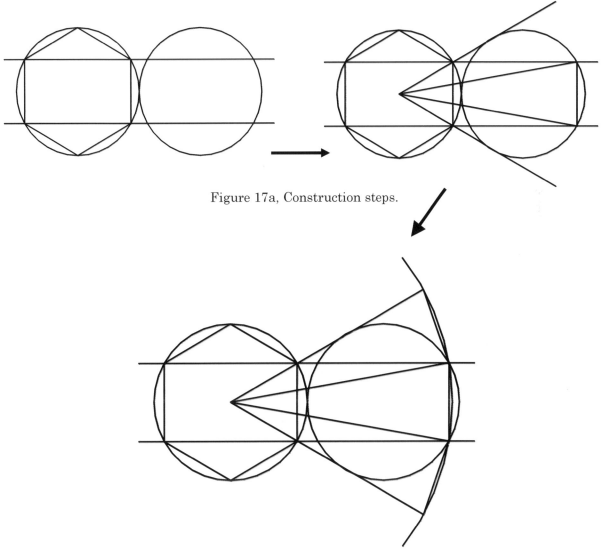

Figure 17a, Construction steps.

Figure 17b, Fairly accurate points for use in 9– and 18– gons.

Figure 18 shows an 18–point geometry, and Figure 19 shows this same geometry overlaid on 12– point, just for an idea (enlarged).

Finally, a number of themes are combined to create the image shown in Figure 20. Geometric art, with a whole lot of hidden Mind behind it all.

Nine. Nine dragons are in Chinese artwork, representing the emperor, but also power and energy, as we have seen earlier in this book. Nine is a number with some primordial significance, supported by the mathematical science we are discovering.

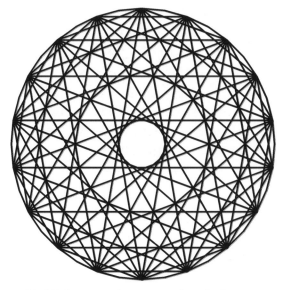

Figure 18, Eighteen points around a circle, connected.

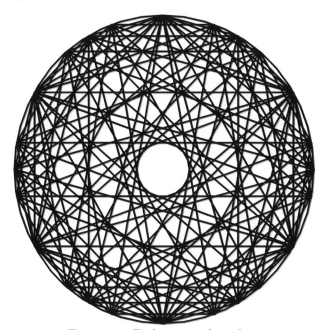

Figure 19, Eighteen and twelve.

Figure 20, Sri Yantra, spirals, and seven.

# Seventh Chapter – Just for fun

**Magic Squares**

Sacred Geometry is "Angelic". This is meant as a facetious reference to Figure 1; where the Archangel Michael is sitting there, compass in hand, as so many of us have done in math class – wondering what it is all about. The title of the print is unfortunately appropriate to most people's math experience: "Melancholia". Dürer's work though is rich in symbolism, like the obvious geometric form, references to time, light, music (tone), and justice. But notice under the bell a table, (enlarged).

Figure 1, Archangel Michael, studying his geometry, surrounded by mathematical objects.

This tabulation contains sixteen numbers, from 1 to 16. Whether or not Dürer intended it, they can be used to create an image. Draw a group of dots, 3 x 3 units on a paper. Imagine that each one represents a number, in sequence. Then, play connect the dot. In Figure 2, this has been done. The left image uses the final line in the table. the right image uses them all.

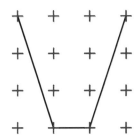
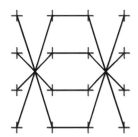

Figure 2, The Dürer "square".

This tabulation is called a "magic square", because the numbers in each row, column, and diagonal add to the same value: in this case 34. Note too how the central four numbers, or four numbers at each corner also add to this value. "Magic".

This is however not the only square which can be generated with sixteen numbers. Figure 3 shows another, with the tabulation given in Table 2.

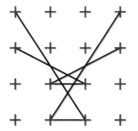 

| 1 | 15 | 14 | 4 |
|---|---|---|---|
| 8 | 10 | 11 | 5 |
| 12 | 6 | 7 | 9 |
| 13 | 3 | 2 | 16 |

Figure 3, Another square of 16 numbers.　　　　Table 1, Numeric arrangement.

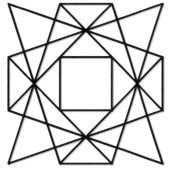 

Figure 4, Images repeated from the sides.

The final process with each of these stars is to count the dots not just top to bottom but from side to side, enabling the images in Figure 4 to be created. Just another way to make exceptional geometry!

A magic square might then consist of any number squared, like 5. Here, in Figure 5, we see the start of something, where a line has been drawn connecting points 1, 24, 3, 23, and 5. The problem here is that we have three numbers from the top and only two from the bottom. Too, the central line is just that, combining 11 thru 15. It's a bit complicated to explain, without doing the math (and that is not the goal of this chapter), that whatever tabulation we attempt with five – square will not result in equal sums. Still, we can follow the pattern at least, to get a very nice image, again ultimately rotated.

Figure 5, The non-magic square of 5. Note the familiar "star" form on the left.

So, the definition of "Magic" square seems to be one which generates a regular pattern in a tabulated form, which then should also make a nice drawing. In Figure 6, we see various attempts with six, all of which though attractive, do not have a tabulation which will result in all rows, columns, and diagonals being equal; basically 1/6th of the total sum of 666.

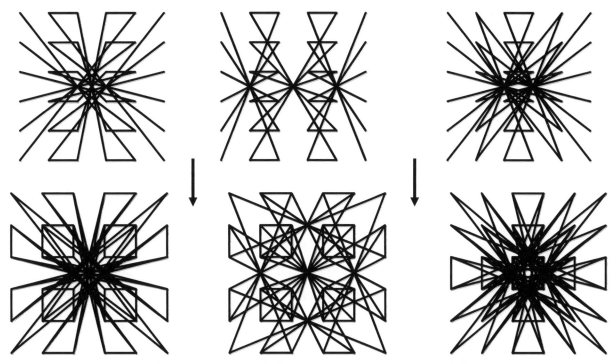

Figure 6a, Drawings made from various tabulations of 6 x 6 (top). Rotated (bottom), but not regular.

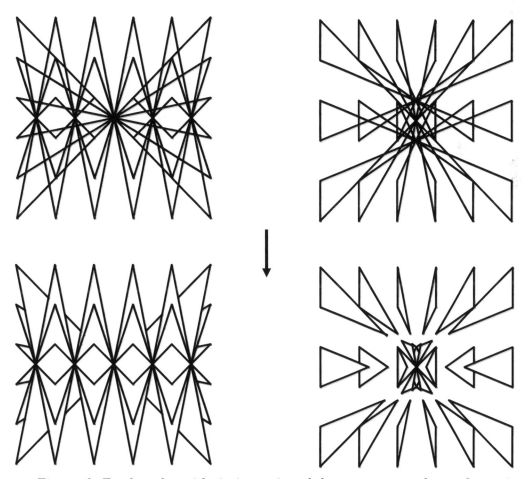

Figure 6b, Further play with six (top set), and then erasure to enhance (bottom).

The number 6 is often associated with the sun, as is 666. A 6 x 6 magic square is esoterically referred to as the square of the sun. Interestingly, in Roman numerals the first six letters (numbers): DCLXVI, total 666. Gematrically, this number has had many associations, ie: Hebraic vaw, vaw, vaw (our WWW).

For god hath put into their hearts to fulfill His will, to give their kingdom unto the beast, that no man might buy or sell, save he that had the mark or the name of the beast or the number of his name. Here is wisdom Let him that hath understanding count the number of the beast, for it is the number of a man; and his number is 666. Book of revelations.

These types of connect-the-dot activities can be fun for people of any age. We can continue, doing diagrams for 7 x 7, as shown in Figure 7. But ultimately, it is when we go into 8 x 8 that we finally reach an excellent drawing, and a regular tabulation (Figure 8 and Table 2).

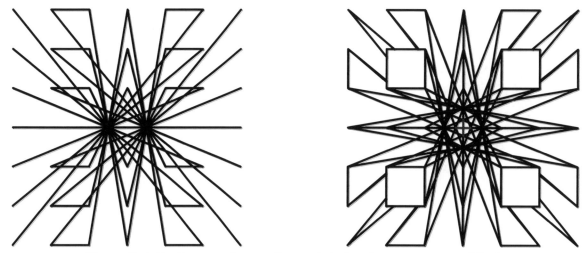

Figure 7, A 7 x 7 square image, then rotated and some erasure. Nice!

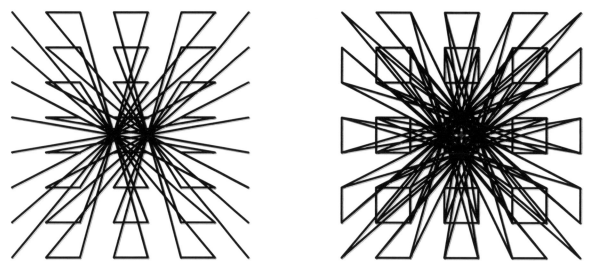

Figure 8, An 8 x 8 square, then rotated. What erasure could enhance these drawings?

| 1 | 63 | 62 | 4 | 5 | 59 | 58 | 8 |
|---|---|---|---|---|---|---|---|
| 16 | 50 | 51 | 13 | 12 | 54 | 55 | 9 |
| 17 | 47 | 46 | 20 | 21 | 43 | 42 | 24 |
| 32 | 34 | 35 | 29 | 28 | 38 | 39 | 25 |
| 40 | 26 | 27 | 37 | 36 | 30 | 31 | 33 |
| 41 | 23 | 22 | 44 | 45 | 19 | 18 | 48 |
| 56 | 10 | 11 | 53 | 52 | 14 | 15 | 49 |
| 57 | 7 | 6 | 60 | 61 | 3 | 2 | 64 |

Table 2, Generation of the 8 x 8 square, which results in a beautiful image; regular.

Finally, we again find a regular pattern; where all rows, columns and diagonals are equal, in the eight x eight square. This is fun, counting, adding, checking and discovering just what will work. As we continue with nine, the following interesting forms appear (Figures 9).

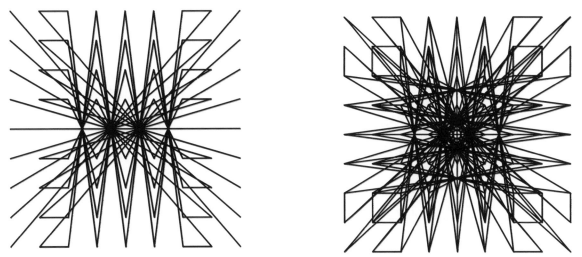

Figure 9a, A 9 x 9 square, then rotated. Now what to erase?

Figure 9b, One attempt at cleaning up the image.

| 1 | 143 | 142 | 4 | 5 | 139 | 138 | 8 | 9 | 135 | 134 | 12 |
|---|-----|-----|-----|-----|-----|-----|-----|-----|-----|-----|-----|
| 24 | 122 | 123 | 21 | 20 | 126 | 127 | 17 | 16 | 130 | 131 | 13 |
| 25 | 119 | 118 | 28 | 29 | 115 | 114 | 32 | 33 | 111 | 110 | 36 |
| 48 | 98 | 99 | 45 | 44 | 102 | 103 | 41 | 40 | 106 | 107 | 37 |
| 49 | 95 | 94 | 52 | 53 | 91 | 90 | 56 | 57 | 87 | 86 | 60 |
| 72 | 83 | 82 | 69 | 68 | 79 | 78 | 65 | 64 | 75 | 74 | 61 |
| 73 | 62 | 63 | 76 | 77 | 66 | 67 | 80 | 81 | 70 | 71 | 84 |
| 85 | 59 | 58 | 88 | 89 | 55 | 54 | 92 | 93 | 51 | 50 | 96 |
| 108 | 38 | 39 | 105 | 104 | 42 | 43 | 101 | 100 | 46 | 47 | 97 |
| 109 | 35 | 34 | 112 | 113 | 31 | 30 | 116 | 117 | 27 | 26 | 120 |
| 132 | 14 | 15 | 129 | 128 | 18 | 19 | 125 | 124 | 22 | 23 | 121 |
| 133 | 11 | 10 | 136 | 137 | 7 | 6 | 140 | 141 | 3 | 2 | 144 |

Table 3, Tabulation of 12 x 12.

127

In Table 3 we see that there is another form that can be made, which is regular; 12 x 12. Actually, as can be seen in the table and the stars shown in Figure 10a and b, this is really repetitive from 8 x 8 and 4 x 4. 6 x 6 has a similar pattern, and the odd numbers in between make a unique addition to the sequence.

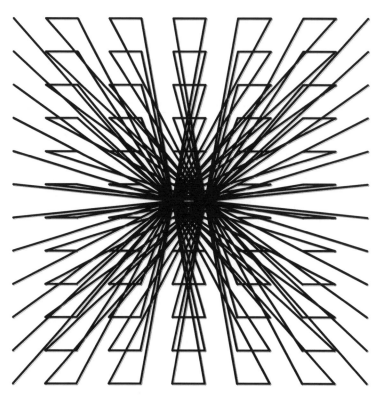

Figure 10a, The 12 x 12 magic square.

Figure 10b, Image rotated. See the color hand-drawing on the back cover for ideas.

Figure 11 A geometric progression of stars.  Cycles of Becoming?

We have seen mathematic rules behind much of what we have drawn in this book, and at least one proportion directly related to biological life.  Could others?  Upon what matrix is life formed?  Is it possible that a tone, a harmonic must be created, presenting a matrix through which cells can grow?  Would such a matrix be random, or regular?

## Lattice structures

We go now to one final use of the straight line; to give the illusion of "curves".  Many are familiar with the rather simple technique of drawing two lines that meet perpendicularly, or at other angles, marking equal spaces along them, and then drawing lines from the marks on one, to marks on the other, working from outside of one to inside on the other, slowly changing toward inside to outside.

A few possibilities are included here, just for reasons of experimentation, which will hopefully be attempted.

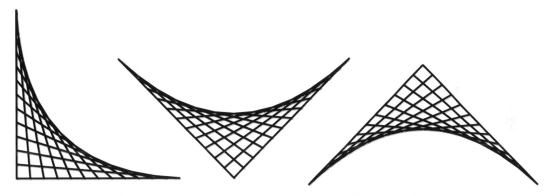

Figure 12, Lattice structures creating a "curved" affect.

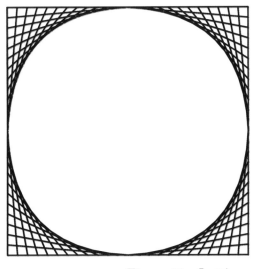

Figure 13a, Lattice square and a "diamond" within.

129

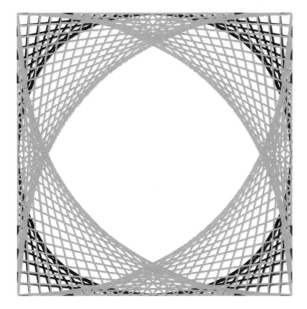

Figure 13b, Lattice squares of two different sizes and colors.

Figure 14, Lattices can be done on circular lines too.

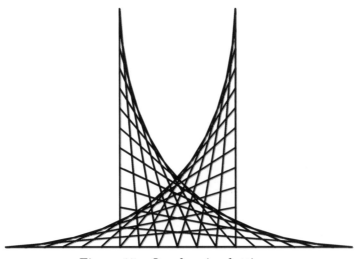

Figure 15a, Overlapping lattices.

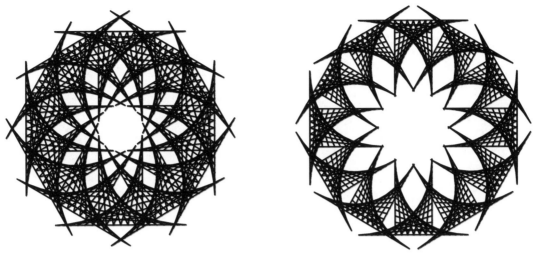

Figure 15b The image repeated in a circle of varying radii.

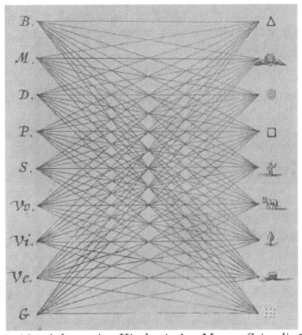

Figure 16a, Athanasius Kircher's Ars Magna Sciendi, 1669.

In Figure 16a we see another avenue upon which we can embark for our lattice structures. Or what of the design in Figure 16b?

Figure 16b, A simple rectangular pattern

Figure 16c, Lattices and loops in a circular form.

We can create the images in Figure 16c by making a circle, and then drawing a series of circles around it, (in a good quantity, such as twelve, eighteen or twenty four) all of a smaller radius that the first. Drawing much smaller circles in the loops, and then some creative erasing, will make the final images as shown. A bit of color and shading can make the image appear 3D.

We cannot emphasize enough that Sacred Geometry must play with a presentation of space; 2D – 3D and 3D – 2D. As we look at an image from afar, or on a flat computer screen, its fullness and depth may only become apparent much closer in, and in a reality that the video display or book cannot convey.

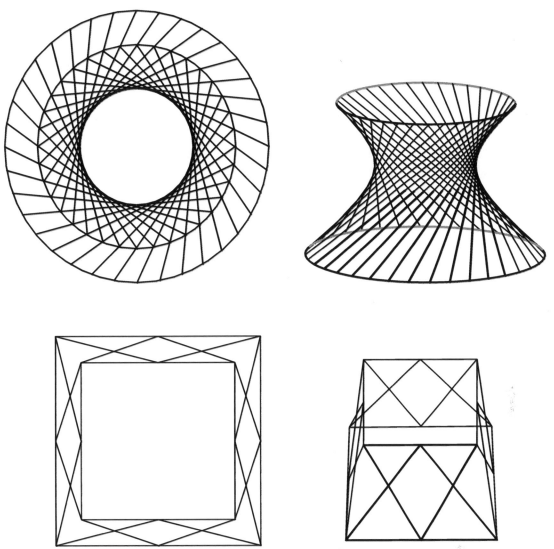

Figure 16d, Lattices as a top view of 3D structures.

As with all of our work, we can ask, is this image truly flat or only a 2D representation of something taking up space?

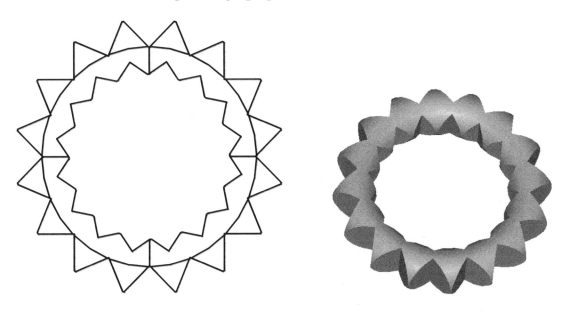

Figure 16e, Mandallic form in 2D of a 3D construction.

## Conclusion; Number

Creating our own Sacred Geometry requires an understanding of the math, an interest in the history, art and architecture, and experience making, measuring, and meditating upon it. Perhaps too, it requires Journey, to Sacred Sites and to Self.

Sacred Geometry is number and pattern, used to describe swirls of energy and the forms they gather into.

Try writing all of the numbers which multiply to make 360; like 1 and 360, 2 and 180... Count the quantity of numbers. There are twelve pairs. Notice the overlay of 12-based counting; 30, 60, 90, etc. with 8-based; 45, 90, 135, etc, and how the two intersect; 90, 180, 270, 360. Twelve and eight (sixteen) based values are a vital part of our angular measurement, astrologos, and system of weights. Their complexity, Sacredness, wisdom, and *relevance* are why the English system **must** survive the press to adopt metrification-simplification.

The values are tabulated here:

| 1 | 2 | 3 | 4 | 5 | 6 | 8 | 9 | 10 | 12 | 15 | 18 |
|---|---|---|---|---|---|---|---|----|----|----|----|
| 360 | 180 | 120 | 90 | 72 | 60 | 45 | 40 | 36 | 30 | 24 | 20 |

Table 1 Factors of 360.

We can learn a lot from this table, by what is present, and missing. In nature and mathematics are many examples of 5 and 6. Ten and twelve based counting are rooted in this, merely complementary-higher harmonics. This is an ancient "rivalry", from at least as far back as Sumer and contemporary Egyptian mathematics. The French revolutionary scientists of the late 18th century resurrected the Egyptian science they were studying and provided us this decimal metric system. In Table 1 we see that the numbers counting to 12 are ten digits, giving an instance of cooperation between the two.

Missing from our ten-of-twelve are 7 and 11. Why are these two considered lucky? Why did the Egyptians use them as the proportion of height-to-base in their greatest pyramid? Why is the slope-length of their second largest pyramid 7x7x7?

We have worked with nearly all of these numerical values to create beautiful imagery, just as Humanity has done for millennia. 360 is key to this work, for the greater quantity of division it provides, or conversely its being the highest harmonic (with 180) of the convergence of the 3-6-12, 4-8-16, 5-10-20, and 9-18-36 streams of growth. 360 is the value by which we measure our year (the Egyptians did, adding five holy days at its end), circles, spheres, *and* squares.

Mythic beliefs have reinforced whatever natural implantation has occurred with these numbers. Sacred Architecture retains their mystery. Within the recesses of the greatest reliquary of Sacred Geometry, the Egyptians used such measures as 9, 10, and 11 (slightly larger than 11); in the so-called "king's" and "queen's" chambers (in addition to other values) which carry interesting combinations on the diagonals, "hidden in plain sight". Interestingly, both the queen's chamber and that under the second pyramid have a vaulted roof which share the *same* height, whose value is nearly perfectly $\sqrt{(\sqrt{2})} \times 10$ cubits (99.97%). See the hypotenuse lengths of 29.5 (moon cycle) and 10Φ which correspond, and the incorporation of $10\sqrt{3}$ and $10\sqrt{5}$ (some exact, others nearly so). Figure 17a. As an aside, the square root of the square root of 2 shows quite a level of mathematical development (if that was the intent)!

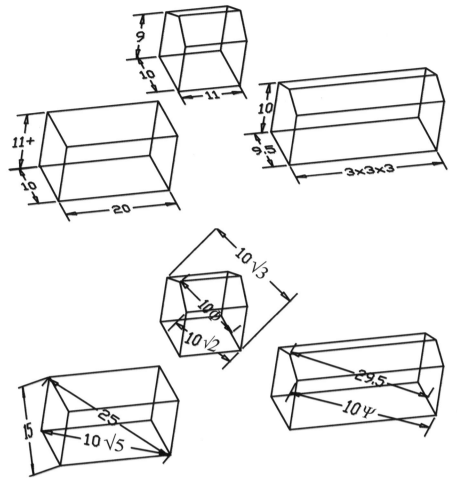

Figure 17a, Lengths in the great chambers.  Note that the slope side of the second pyramid is 7x7x7.

Sacred Geometry includes values we have no modern relation to; like a furlong of 11x60 feet (660), or 11x40 (440); the length of the base of the Great Pyramid. This is also the length of the diagonal of the plane upon which the king's chamber sits.  So, this room's altitude had to be carefully laid out.  Of note, this plane is also the volumetric midpoint for the structure.  See that the King's chamber is situated away from the center and how it specifically misses the crossing lines of the pyramid.  According to "Feng Shui"?  Location.

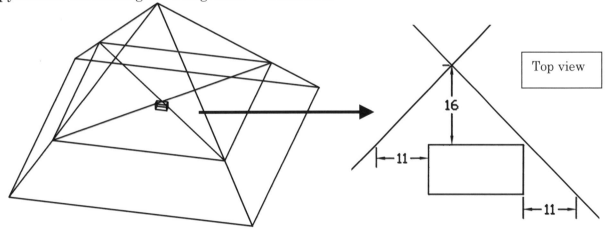

Figure 17b, Location of the King's chamber.  Diagonals here equal ground base length.

Sacred Geometry includes the irrational; √2, √3, and √5 as found within these pyramids, and also the regular forms we have studied.  It includes phi, psi, and other strange numbers; known and those yet to be (re)discovered.  And 15-20-25 is a 3-4-5 pythagorean triangle!

## Conclusion; Wave

The concept of Sacred Geometry is birthed of light and sound, both of which create geometric matrices. Some minerals, cellular creatures, and snowflakes form accordingly. Bees build with this.

> In the beginning God created the heaven and the earth... And God said, Let there be light: and there was light... And God made two great lights; the greater light to rule the day, and the lesser light to rule the night... Genesis

> In the beginning was the Word, and the Word was with God, and the Word was God... In him was life; and the life was the light of men...That was the true Light, which lighteth every man that cometh into the world.... John

See in Figure 18a the interference pattern in water from two rocks hitting the surface simultaneously. Light going through a double slit behaves this way. But how do single source waves interact in 3D space? Here, nodes also form, as shown in Figure 19. Musical notes and visible colors are thought to reach into 3D spherical space according to the Platonic and other forms. Are these a matrix for life? Is it one which determines energetic power points on a planetary surface?

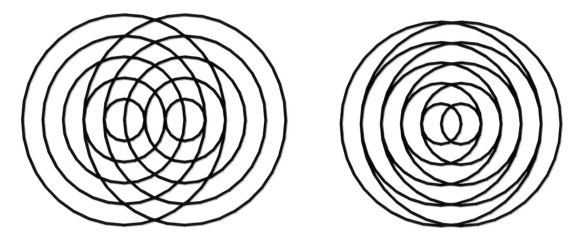

Figure 18a, Interference patterns, random spacing on impulses and one according to Vesica piscis

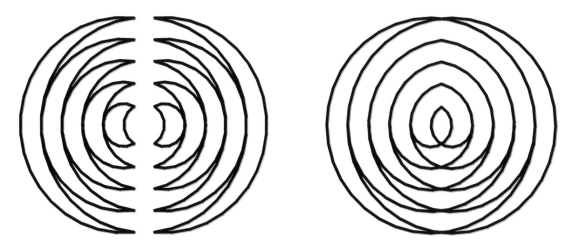

Figure 18b, Play, as always, with the forms drawn.

136

Figure 19a, 2D image of a sound wave. Note the star tetrahedron, Cymatic image ©2001 MACROmedia Publishing, Used by permission.

Figure 19b, Octahedral shape found in fluorite, diamond (USGS), and electron shells.

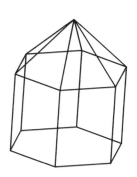  

Figure 19c, Hexagonal form in crystals, Giant's causeway (M. Mayer), and Garnet (USGS).

 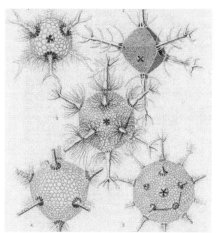

Figure 19d, Radiolariens, as regular and Platonic forms (Ernst Haeckel 1862).

137

## Conclusion; Architecture

We can find the Sacred all around us. As expressions of the Creator, we must remember, that which comes from our hands is also sacred. After all, we too are the Sacred. We have the laws of the universe written in our body, the forms of Plato, the 5-pointed star, nature (at the minutest levels), and key mathematics.

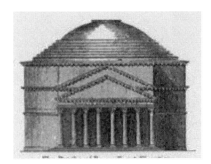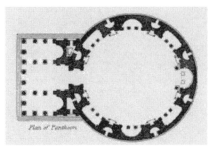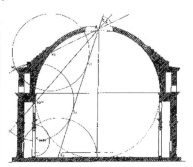

Figure 20a, Geometry in the round. The Pantheon (A. Desdogetz 1779)

Figure 20b, The Heavans. The blue mosque (Travis Reitter).

Figure 20c, The Taj Mahal, and inlay of precious stones (Dhirad and wiki).

The architectural relics of earlier ages show Humanities' interest in creating edifices of beauty which would endure. "Frozen Music". Contained within these wonders is science, mathematics (both concrete), and symbolism which we are left to decipher.

138

Figure 21, Geometry in linear. The Parthenon, known for its phi proportions.

Figure 22, One of the wheels of the chariot, for a Hindu solar temple (G.-U. Tolkiehn).

Figure 23, Sacred landscape and the temple, Angkor Wat (Charles J Sharp and wiki).

What is the architectural plan upon which the structure is made? What geometry does it contain? As the structure rises up from this foundation, what do the walls, and roof convey? Could it be of not one, but of several heavens (perhaps 9) which rise above our heads (Figure 20b)?

See in Figure 22 the temple of Surya, the sun god, at Konark India. The entire temple is as a chariot, with twelve dharma wheels (each of eight spokes), pulled by seven great horses. A typical Hindu temple, it is covered in erotic art, for all to see. In this culture the Sacred includes Sacred Sex.

Figure 23 shows the landscaping, and inclusion of the elements, incorporated in Angkor Wat. This site is thought to be representative of the Hindu universe; concentric islands around Mt. Meru.

## Conclusion; Math reflecting Nature

The Sacred which is found in Geometry is our Human understanding of the Mind involved with Creation. There is Harmony in Geometry. There is tone, distance, rhythm, and time.

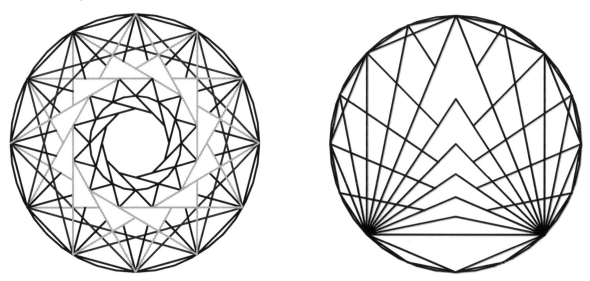

Figure 24a, Further ideas of things we can create.

Figure 24b, Reflection in nature.

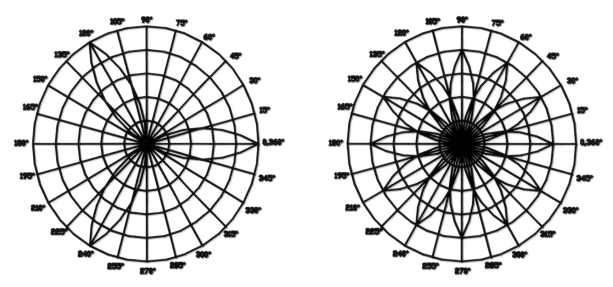

Figure 25, Cosine functions placed on a polar rather than rectangular graph. Change in perspective changes the appearance of the function, recreating our daisy patterns. Geometry hidden in nature.

140

Before the time of the industrial revolution, true education (education being that in which a much smaller portion of the general populace could participate) taught the Renaissance Man (Woman being part of the exclusion) a great deal about the microcosmos and macrocosmos. While it wasn't available to the masses, it was much more detailed than the standardized, mass production of Today; sanitized of the Sacred, the universal, in favor of creating people who can be "plugged in" somewhere.

Figure 26, The students of Sacred Geometry – School of Athens by Raphael.

What more is there for us to learn? How can our educational processes vitalize, and help each person to their destiny?

Today a fog of distraction envelopes us all, from a barrage of electronic radiation, explosion of information, and enrapture with media in all its forms. The strength of learning perhaps peaked in the 17th and 18th centuries among the great minds of Bacon, Culpepper, Goethe, Kepler, and the Rosicrucians, Qabbalists, Alchemists, Astrologers, and other mystery schools of the middle ages (though kept alive by Blavatsky, Steiner, and others in more modern times). We see their Creation in the Baroque Art and Architecture of Europe, paralleled by contemporary Hindu, Buddhist, and Islamic efforts; unequalled by the glass, steel, and concrete of the Modern. A culmination of intuitive study of millennia vs. objective Science of a few centuries. Mind without heart, or gut.

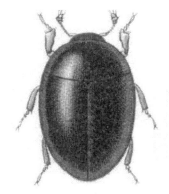

Figure 27a, Symmetrical geometry (Käfer des deutschen Reiches, Reitter 1908; KD Harrelson).

141

Figure 27b, Mandala found in Passion flower and dandelion (Tomas Castelazo and kendra/wiki).

What can we find intuitively, and observationally? The images in Figures 27 show how nature can be a guide. See the regular geometric patterns in flowers and animal life. Symmetry. Note the sphere formed by the lowly dandelion, or the sun burst of its blossom. Light and sound spread in this fashion. How might *we* be the light, and bring light to others?

Figure 27c, Dandelion blossom. Snapping turtle. Notice the hexagonal plates (wiki).

What messages are we able to receive from the ancient philosopher-scientist-priest? What grains do we find uniquely *and* universally in varied mystery paths?

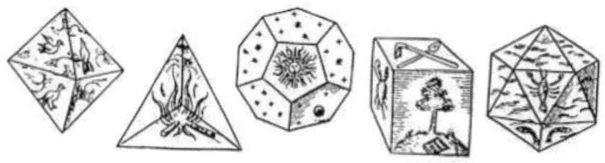

Figure 28, The elements and Platonic forms (Kepler).

Perhaps we should not be too right-brain as Moderns. Maybe we can find a way to look at things intuitively, again value things subjectively, and use something other than technology to find all of our solutions.

## Conclusion; Astro-Logos

By what mechanics is the great disparity in size coordinated with an equally great proportional difference in distance, such that Sun and Moon, the "rulers" of day and night appear equal in size in our sky? By what mechanics is the time of Moon's rotation on its axis such that it always shows us the same face?

 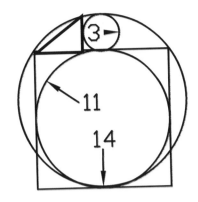

Figure 29a, Solar eclipse (Luc Viatour)   29b, Relative sizes of Moon (radius 3) and Earth (11), and the circle and square determined by them (sharing an equal perimeter). Notice the triangle is 3-4-5!

There is no accident that we may represent the relative spacing of planets in their orbits on each joint of our hand, or find in fractal images the distances between planets, and their relative sizes.

In only the last few years, Astro-namers have discovered many more bodies beyond the orbit of Pluto. On the one hand, this has helped us understand the cloud of matter (and Spirit?), which is gathered around our solar system; while on the other it has been determined to downgrade these "planetoids"; Pluto included.

The astrological glyphs for the planets were derived by the alchemical arts and therefore have great symbolic meaning. Each consists of O, ☾, and/or +. These could be thought to represent Sun, Moon and Earth; fire, water, and earth; or thought/spirit, emotion/soul, and matter/form (among other things). The planetary glyphs are combinations of these three.

Circles, crosses, and crescents (and spirals) have been found at historic sites from the dawn of civilization. Human art and symbolism buried in our genetic psyche for millennia.

Venus with its circle above the cross could indicate spirit above matter ♀ (Relationship). The arrow of Mars is a portion of the cross, tugging at the spirit: Activation ♂. The symbol of Mercury is like that of Venus, but with a crescent atop it, indicating moon – soul. Soul and Spirit above matter – Mind. Earth; matter contained within spirit, or spirit encompassing body. Jupiter; soul and matter together. Saturn; Matter over soul, the difficulty associated with this planet. Neptune, the dreaminess of matter underneath soul, as our bodies sleep and our spirit journeys. Notice the interaction of soul, spirit, and matter in the glyphs for Mercury, Uranus and Pluto.

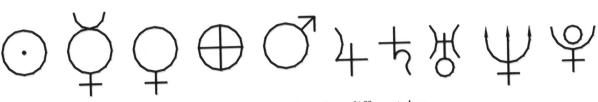

Figure 30, Glyphs given in a different Age.

What deeper meaning was intended by the Alchemist – Astrologer? What did they understand of the spacing of the planets – the "music of the spheres"? What signs could we assign to the newly discovered orbs?

Figure 31, The cosmic dance of Shiva, in creation and destruction (he stands upon ignorance) (wiki).

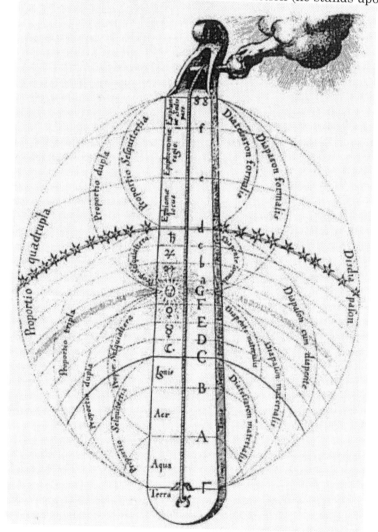

Figure 32 Fractions and Music (From Fludd's De Musica Mundana).

Whose is The Hand? What can *our* hands also create? The drawings, forms, structures we build can all be based on Sacredness, instead of lifeless printouts and boxes. Certainly the children which come from us are physical models of this, just as their ancestors were. Create the Sacred, that which gives awe.

144

## Conclusion; Spiral

In Figure 33 we return to twelve-fold division, drawing 12 phi spirals, which are then mirrored. The beautiful geometry of the flower, containing the life spark, which carries forward the species.

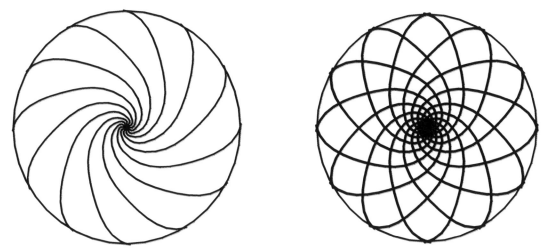

Figure 33, Play with phi, and 12.

We are awash in a sea of energy; flowing, pulsing, expanding-contracting, breathing in and out. Geometric form, architecture, and crystals are a frozen form of this. Press a crystal, heat it, and energy flows. Likewise, it is an antenna – probably sensed by the megalith builders of our ancient past. Crystals are found in great quantity in our bodies, particularly in the brain. Though microscopic they certainly form regular shapes. They are our link, or connection between mind and blood, external sensation and internal impulse. Sacred geometry tunes them.

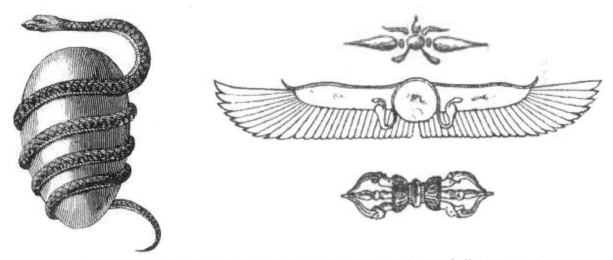

Figure 34a, The Orphic Egg (Manly Hall – Secret Teachings of all Ages 1928)
Figure 34b, Energy (The Migration of Symbols – Goblet d'Alviella 1894)

The egg, spiral, and Energy are all related, in form, conception, and vibration. Regeneration. Flow.

For so long metaphysical sciences have been hidden from us, in plain sight. They are there for us, waiting like apples to be plucked from the tree of knowledge. We must take the time, and slow down, in order that we might learn. Breathe.

Sacred Geometry *is* number and pattern which describes swirls of energy; coming into Being. Let's finish by looking at the Spiral, and counting with it through our chakras, thinking deeply upon each number.

| Symbol | Label |
|--------|-------|
| | Completion |
| | Form |
| | Life |
| | Space |
| | Time |
| | Energy |
| | Source |

Figure 35, Spirals in the sea (Ernst Haeckel 1904), and a different way to count.

One is the Source. Self. Creator. Two is the flow of energy, between Self and Creator, and Self; high and low, low and high, day-night-day, summer-winter-summer, etc. Three is energy in motion, or time. Four is space created. With five imagine all we have seen with phi: Life! Six is form, in all of the many two and three dimensional patterns we've studied. And Seven is completion. Though in some ways unique, 8 and 9 are in other ways just higher vibrations of 2 and 3.

I am the eternal...I am Ra... I am that which created the word... I am the word – The Egyptian book of the Dead, also called the book of coming into the Light.

The Word (tone) is a complex wave of mixing-different frequencies, which applied on various materials take on specific patterns and forms. Frequencies of sound and light also create different forms. All work through Resonance (that similar energy patterns, movement, and shape create exchange of energy and information) and Harmonics (the octaves, or dimensional levels, of vital energy).

Humanity has used the Word (number) in 60 centuries of their architectural development. Our astro –, alchemical – , medicinal – , and metaphysical – sciences were once built according to the same models we have seen demonstrated in these chapters. Modern specialization has taken us far from our roots, while admittedly expanding our knowledge. Yet many are seeking a return to Balance.

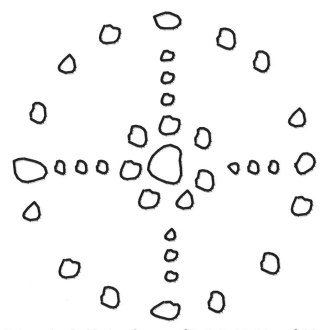

Figure 37, Ojibwa medicine wheel. Notice the use of 3, 4, 7, 12, 16, and 36. Imagine making this, with rocks, crystals, or candles.

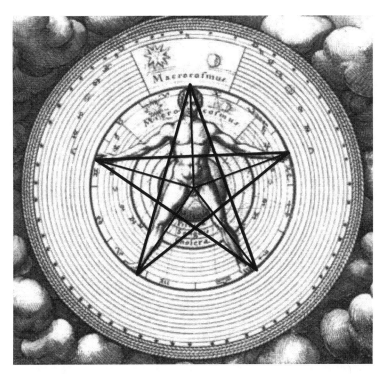

Figure 38, Meditational pose, focused on the lower chakras (modified- Cosmi Ultriusque – R. Fludd).

## Meditation

As we enter into creation of our own Sacred Geometry, and transition in Life which proceeds from this, we might at times wish to pause and go inward. The following is offered as one further meditational form:

Begin by preparing your self and space. Turn off electro magnetic equipment around you, particularly wireless devices. Open the windows if you can, or better go under Solar, Lunar, or Forest roof. Light a candle or fire. Make a circle, perhaps as shown in Figure 37. If you like, prepare yourself with yoga or Qi gong.

Figure 39, What Sacred Space, and atmosphere, can you create? (John William Waterhouse).

Sit comfortably, or stand (perhaps in the geometry suggested in Figures 38 and 40). Focus on your root chakra – feel the ground. Imagine the gems Garnet, or a finely worked ruby. Imagine a cone of energy spiraling into you from the Earth. See it form as a red tetrahedron, or the four – petalled flower. Visualize thin white streams of energy connecting your root to the red center of the earth. If you have a bell, brass bowl, crystal glass, drum, or something tonal, strike it and simply breathe. Draw energy from Earth. You are already long since energetically linked, for without this there is no life. Hum or sing very lowly, "uuu".

Orange is the color of the sex chakra. This is very needful of being clear. Not only are the sexual energies between the genders most difficult to harmonize, but this is one chakra which may be under particular assault today as there are those who think its vibrations are in the microwave region – the realm of almost all modern forms of communication. Human reproduction and health of our children are desperately at risk. Think on an octahedron or a six – petalled flower, and the three axis contained within both. Remember the ways to create an octahedron; the transformations. Imagine atom, cell, reproductivity, and health. See the beauty of citrine. Bring body, soul, and spirit into harmony. Sing "ohh".

Imagine as we progress through the chakras of what frequency vibrations they might contain and how to balance them. Think too as we color our images, how to use color to heal ourselves, and if we prefer one color what this may say about us. How do we bring balance?

148

Yellow, the solar plexus. The Will. Gold. Connect to Sun. Lay under Sun and feel the warmth within your body. Heal your Will, and your liver; give up the food and drink which quash it. Imagine an icosahedron here; phi − complexity. Conversely, imagine the ten − petalled flower, containing two pentagons. Remember how our essence relates to phi. Find inside what you desire in life. Let your imagination create a picture of this. Breathe and release it to create itself of its own. Do not receive impressions from outside that you do not want. Develop "Soul armor" an energy layer around yourself. Sing "oww".

Figure 40, Four (of many) possible poses during meditation.

Green is the color of Nature, and the Heart. Mentally place a Merkaba, or star tetrahedron here. Imagine one yellow tetrahedron rotating counter-clockwise, drawing Earth's energy upward. The second, which is blue, turns opposite, drawing down cosmic energies. Their fusion, whose internal structure is an octahedron, is green, as the colors mix. Connect the Will and the Word. What Good can we thus bring to our World, our relationships? Love the land, our Mother and yet older sister, above which shines our older brother. We cannot return to the womb, to the embrace; certainly not since our splitting of the atom. No, we as a species have attained adolescence, perhaps some early adulthood. We must change our thinking to one more adult in orientation; finding a way in which to work more cooperatively than presently. Conversely to the Merkaba, think of a twelve − petalled flower, containing two hexagons. Imagine all the ways that the two relate. Open our hearts, heal the old wounds, learn to Love again. Love Earth, each other, and all Children. Protect them. Strive to live in harmony, with nature and spirit. Cultivate perseverance, tolerance of others, and trust in the phenomena around us. Sing "ay" (like hey).

Blue is the color of the globe surrounding us (held up by the might of Atlas), water which reflects its greatness, and the throat chakra. Lift our gaze to the blue sky, opening up this chakra. Let's focus on the cube, its square faces/eight corners, and the four (7) directions. Sing "ah", as you strike your musical instrument. Hope that as you open this chakra you may be gifted with the Words best used in your relationships, that your ears truly listen and hear. Remember that in the beginning was the Word. Pray that you may taste well of life. Following the model from the East, we can also consider the sixteen – petalled flower. What do we now know about 4 – 8 – 16? Put consciousness and meaning into our decisions and speech.

The third eye, the brow. Two lotus petals in a flower, like wings. Open up our true seeing, beyond the media which we are so much allowing to influence and block our thoughts and visions, our dreaming in color, and our ability to see the angelic realms. Imagine stellating the icosahedron. Put an amethyst here, strike the gong again, and breathe. Focus always on the ideas which come to our mind. Release those which have no meaning. Learn as much as we can. Sing "ee".

Place a diamond, flourite, or clear quartz crystal, atop your head, your crown. Imagine. Let the cosmic forces enter through this crystal. Focus on a dodecahedron (which Plato associated with the Cosmos), or the spider's web geometry of a thousand interweaving lines, all streaming down from the cosmos. Then, clear your mind of all thought, of this entire meditation. Breathe. Connect to the realm of Spirit. Let your soul open to God. Sing "I".

Imagine energy flowing upward from Earth, through your body, through each energized chakra, sprouting out of your crown and then showering down around you, around and through your auric field. Connect with the free energy that Tesla and Reich have each determined to be around us.

Chant, "May I be ready to receive what I am next to receive".
"Heal my Body, heal my Karma, heal my Body, heal my Spirit"

Breathe.

Create the sacred; that which gives awe. Create symbols which represent visible images of higher spiritual processes. Live life as an image of your relationship to higher worlds.

Begin to draw Mandala. Begin your day. Or go to sleep now and enjoy dreams which are different. Thus let the light shine, the bell to ring.

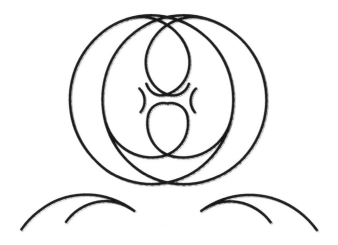

Be a Light, like a crystal; a conduit for positive, peace, energy.

## About the Author

Paul Stang is a teacher, student, and artist of Sacred Geometry, Mathematics, Astrology, Archaeo-Astronomy, Leylines and Sciences. His initial education and career was in Aviation Engineering, where he saw first-hand application of mathematics. His second education came from the Earth spirits of the American West, and then the Minds of ancient architects from around the world, doing odd-jobs along the way; managing a medicinal herbal company, assisting the engineer on an environmental boat, and building houses. Basically, "vision quest", though unknown at the time.

Coincidental to obtaining an advanced degree in Arts he began a new career in teaching. Each summer travel season continued to imbue new inspirations into his efforts, both artistic and practical. He has taught an ever-growing range of materials internationally at high school, university, and adult workshops.

Specific themes presented, taught, or published to date include "Using Mandalas in Mathematics Instruction", "2 and 3 Dimensional Constructions", "Zometools in the Creative Classroom", "Phi - The Golden Section", "In the Footsteps of the Masters – Stonehenge, Pyramids and da Vinci", "I as Symbol in the Circle of Life", "Rocketry for Physics and Mathematics Lessons", "The Historical Development of Alchemy as a Means of Teaching Chemistry", "Wiccan Mathematics? – Yes!", and "Theatrical Presentation of Mathematics".

He currently lives in the Czech Republik, attempting to find now cosmic voices. Find out more on his website:

http://www.mysterymath.info/  Or email him at paulstang@gmail.com

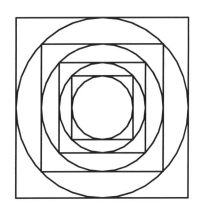

## Bibliography

### Books

Michael Schneider, A beginner's guide to constructing the Universe, 1994 , HarperCollins New York

Bruce Rawles, Sacred Geometry Design Sourcebook., 1997 Elysian Publishing

Gerald S. Hawkins, Stonehenge Decoded, 1965, Doubleday and Company, New York

Robert Gilbert, PhD.  Egyptian and European Energy Work, 2005, Vesica LLC

John Martineau, A little book of Coincidences in the Solar System, 2001, Wooden Books

Sir Norman Lockyer, Dawn of Astronomy, 1894, Macmillan, New York

Sir Norman Lockyer, Stonehenge and other British stone Monuments, astronomically considered, 1906,

W. M. Flinders Petrie, The Pyramids and Temples of Gizeh, 1883

John Michell, The view over Atlantis, 1969

John Michell, City of Revelation, 1972

Zecharia Sitchin, When Time Began, 1993, Avon Books

Alchemy & Mysticism, the Hermetic Museum, Alexander Roob, 2001

Rudolf Steiner, How to know Higher worlds, Anthroposophic Press, 1994

Richard Stang, Journeys through Earth time, Creative Communications, 1994

Manly Hall, Secret Teachings of all Ages, 1928


### Websites:

http://www.Wikipedia

www.cymaticsource.com        MACROmedia Publishing, Newmarket NH  03857  USA

http://www.sacred-texts.com/

## Other books by Paul

## "I had fun in Mr. Stang's math class!"

Imagine your child, and you, enjoying mathematics. '**We as Architects in the Wheel of Life**' is about You! – answering the question "Why do we study Math?" '**Mathematics that is alive, artistic, applied**' is written by a teacher fortunate to have taught 15 years at independent schools, free from standardization and technology – modern 'pillars' that dilute the real meaning while profitting those who sell such things. Every person is intelligent, and when that is tapped, they find their own understanding of Math

This book is holistic education; marrying art, science, hands-on activities – all to inspire the creative teacher, homeschooler and enthusiast. It further discusses important social issues.

Excellent for late primary, highschool and university levels; a premier book written by one of the most creative algebra, geometry and trig teachers on the planet.

More about books, art, creative math, and workshops at http://mysterymath.wordpress.com

**The Forest of Dlahomila** is a wonderful children's fairytale about Faeries and Gnomes and the world they inhabit.

At first the two have a great distrust for each other but come to find that they are really not so different and even become friends.

Full of beautiful artwork, mischief, and morals. Great for bedtime stories.

**Meditation to Activate your Chakras and Cleanse your Auric Layers** is the first of a series of three booklets which came out as a result of Exploring the Sacred and are meant as the next evolution. Within are great color paintings, some inspired by Barbara Brennan's much more extensive work. These small guides are for you to create your own healing and energizing, as you 'raise your vibration', working with the **seven rays** towards your own **Ascension**.

Mathematics Discovery Activities

For Children ages 4 to 11

**Mathematics Discovery Activities** is a compilation of guided projects ideally suited for homeschooling parents and creative teachers of math, for small children.

Paul Stang, MA

By Paul Stang, MA

Made in the USA
Monee, IL
25 May 2021